Innovations in Advocacy and Empowerment for People with Intellectual Disabilities

Lisieux Hall Publications

Innovations in Advocacy and Empowerment for People with Intellectual Disabilities

Published by:

Lisieux Hall Publications, Whittle-le-Woods, Chorley, Lancashire, England PR6 7DX

Copyright © Lisieux Hall Publications, 1998

A catalogue entry for this book is available from the British Library.

ISBN 1-870335 2 4 4

Cartoons:

Unless otherwise stated, the cartoons are by Angela Martin.

Acknowledgements

Thanks to the Joseph Rowntree Foundation for contributing financial support; to Maggi Walton for her good humoured typing and re-typing of chapter drafts; and to colleagues at the Norah Fry Research Centre for their support and their continuing commitment to the empowerment of people with learning difficulties

Innovations in Advocacy and Empowerment for People with Intellectual Disabilities

Edited by

Linda Ward

Lisieux Hall Publications

Recent Publications available from Lisieux Hall

Innovations in Health Care for People with Intellectual Disabilities
edited by Michael Kerr

Presents an up-to-date review of best practice in the delivery of health care and advances in medical science.

Innovations in Evaluating Services for People with Intellectual Disabilities edited by Roy McConkey.

The international authorship make this one of the most comprehensive and up-to-date reviews on current thinking about service evaluation. Essential reading for planners and managers.

Innovations in Developing Countries for People with Disabilities, edited by Brian O'Toole and Roy McConkey.

This important collection of essays ... will provide CBR planners and workers with insight into the rich diversity of CBR initiatives and the importance of leadership and activism by disabled people. Health Rights

Innovations in Family Support for People with Learning Disabilities, edited by Peter and Helle Mittler.

This book is a must for all professionals working in the field. It will become a key reference volume in the area of family studies. Frontline

Innovations in Educating Communities about Learning Disabilities, edited by Roy McConkey.

Two features distinguish this addition to the campaigning literature; the selection of often telling cartoons and the emphasis on supporting people with disability labels to be their own ambassadors. Care Weekly

Innovations in Educating Children with Severe Learning Disabilities, edited by John Harris.

It is rare to read a book about the national curriculum and children with severe learning disabilities that is readable and practical. But this is one such book.
Care Weekly

Innovations in Employment Training and Work for People with Learning Difficulties, edited by Roy McConkey & Patrick McGinley.

Useful practical guide to a number of innovative programmes in vocational training and employment in the UK and other countries.
Mental Handicap Research

For my Father

Cyril Ward

(1904-1997)

Innovations in Advocacy and Empowerment for People with Intellectual Disabilities

Contents

Foreword

Marcia Rioux and Barb Goode

This book is about advocacy but it also about partnership.

❖ It is about people with intellectual disabilities making their voices heard – and about other people (their supporters, families, friends, people in their communities) helping this happen.

❖ It is about people with intellectual disabilities making their views known – and about other people listening and helping things to change.

❖ It is about individual people with intellectual disabilities being supported to make choices and changes in their own lives.

❖ It is about groups of people with intellectual disabilities coming together to support each other and to have a say in the policies and practices which affect their daily lives.

❖ It is about everyone – men and women, children, adults and older people, from all ethnic groups and backgrounds, people with profound and multiple disabilities, people who may have additional mental health or other problems.

There is a wide range of things covered by advocacy and this book reflects that variety. The contributions to it are co-written or inspired by people with intellectual disabilities and their allies, not just in the United Kingdom but in the United States, Australia and Canada too.

We as writers of this foreword have our own *her*story of partnership. As a women with an intellectual disability, Barb Goode has a long herstory of involvement in the self-advocacy movement worldwide. Marcia Rioux too, as President of Canada's Roeher Institute, has a long-standing herstory of involvement and support in their struggle for equal citizenship for people with intellectual disabilities generally.

We have both been involved in the process of re-shaping the goals and objectives of the community living movement in Canada. More famously perhaps, we shared involvement in the celebrated legal case 'About Eve' where we fought for the rights of women with intellectual disabilities not to be sterilised without their consent.

In the past few years, we and others of our friends, have worked together to put books that are important to people's lives into plain language, for example, books on money.

And we both continue to be involved in the international movement for advocacy and change through *Inclusion International* (formerly the International League of Societies for Persons with Mental Handicap).

The struggle for equal citizenship for people with intellectual disabilities is not yet won. This wider struggle is made up of many smaller scale struggles which are of huge significance in the daily lives of individual people with intellectual disabilities in their homes, their neighbourhoods and their countries. We are proud to play our part in this struggle and contribute this foreword to a book which gives many accounts of practical ways to bring about change which we hope will inspire readers to take actions of their own. As Barb said when she became the first person with an intellectual disability to address the General Assembly of the United Nations.

Our voice may be a new one to many of you but you should better get used to hearing it.

Many of us still have to learn how to speak up.

Many of you still have to learn how to listen to us and how to understand us.

We demand that you give us the right to make choices and decisions regarding our own lives.

We are tired of people telling us what to do what they want. Instead let us all work together as a team!

Reference

Goode, B. (1992) Address to the U.N. General Assembly. *ILSMH News, 14,* Brussels, ILSMH (now Inclusion International)

Section 1
Introduction

1 Voices and Choices

Innovations in Advocacy and Empowerment - an overview

Linda Ward

London, 1996. The Mental Health Foundation is launching the report of its Committee of Enquiry into services for people with learning difficulties in the UK (Mental Health Foundation, 1996). The launch is attended by key figures in the world of policy and practice in this area, along with representatives of the media. It is addressed by Dame Gillian Wagner. And the other keynote speaker? Richard West, a young man with learning difficulties and a hearing impairment who has been involved with colleagues from CHANGE (an organisation of people with learning difficulties and additional impairments) in preparing a user-friendly version of the report for people with learning difficulties themselves. He addresses the audience via a sign language interpreter ...

Bristol, 1997. The Strathcona Theatre Group, a group of actors with learning difficulties, are touring the UK with their production 'Error of Judgement'. It deals powerfully with issues of abuse and harassment. Wherever the play tours, workshops are held, attended by people with learning difficulties from the locality. Accessible, user-friendly resources are available, so that the lessons of the play can be carried through into people's everyday lives.

January, 1998. A report is launched on Independent Visitors and disabled young people (Knight, 1998a). The Children Act 1989 requires local authorities in the UK to appoint Independent Visitors for children and young people who are looked after by them and have had little or no contact with their parents for at least twelve months. The research shows that a large proportion of local authorities are still not using Independent Visitors but where they are, the effect can be enormous.

> *Liz, for example, is fifteen and has lived in a residential unit for five years with no contact with her family. Because she has autism and some challenging behaviour, a social worker has discounted the possibility of her moving to live with a family. But, Vivien, her Independent Visitor has been having her home for tea once a fortnight for about six months. Liz has enjoyed mixing with Vivien's three children and has not displayed any difficult behaviour. As a result, social services start looking into the possibility of finding a family placement for Liz ...*

> *In the same study, two other Independent Visitors act as advocates for other young people with severe learning difficulties, when it becomes clear through the deterioration of their behaviour they are unhappy where they are living. Both volunteers meet with social services staff to discuss the situations and one young person subsequently moves to a smaller home, more geared to her needs.*
> (from Knight, 1998a)

All these, and many more, are examples of advocacy and empowerment for people with learning difficulties in the UK today. Advocacy, empowerment, user involvement ... They are all buzz words in the 1990s but experience, research and the examples quoted in the chapters that make up this volume testify that these are more than buzz words alone. For many people with learning difficulties in the UK and elsewhere, advocacy and empowerment are making a real difference to the quality of their lives.

It is impossible to do justice to the rich variety of innovations in advocacy and empowerment for people with learning difficulties in one volume. But what follows is a powerful illustration of the multiplicity of initiatives that are underway. All, however, have some things in common. They present positive pictures of what is possible, even when they are set against a backdrop of the overwhelming need for change in the conditions of people's lives. They are practical and easily transferable or adaptable to individual readers' local circumstances. They embrace many different aspects of the lives of people with learning difficulties and those involved with them.

About the Book

The book is divided into five sections. This section **(Section 1)** provides an introduction to the book overall. It places each of the contributions into some kind of context and looks a little more closely at two areas which are not covered in any detail elsewhere in the volume: issues around advocacy and involvement for disabled children and young people and the involvement of people with learning difficulties in research and evaluation.

Section 2: Coming Together for Change presents three different accounts of the importance of collective action in bringing about change for people with learning difficulties. 'One Day At a Time: Changing a System to Realise a Dream' describes how Ray Browning was empowered to bring about changes in his life, with the help of a variety of different allies whom he enlisted in his support. It is followed by a chapter co-written by Bridget Whittell and Paul Ramcharan and members of People First, Cardiff and the Vale in Wales, which presents their experiences developing self-advocacy in their area. In the final chapter of the section, Hank Bersani Jr., looks back at the development of the international self-advocacy movement, from its origins in social clubs (where young people with learning difficulties were able to meet together) to a genuine social movement for change.

A key demand of the self-advocacy movement has been for accessible information. **Section 3: Information for Empowerment** describes different ways in which the quest for accessible information has been taken forward. In Chapter 5: 'Information is Power', Ruth Townsley describes the *Plain Facts* initiative: a series of accessible, user-friendly magazines on paper and audio-tape, presenting the findings from research projects in ways that are useful to people with learning difficulties themselves. Miriam Ticoll in 'Working Together for Change', recounts how The Roeher Institute, Canada's leading public policy research institute has tackled the challenge of ensuring meaningful involvement of people with intellectual disabilities in their work. Back in the UK, Jeannie Sutcliffe and Richard West's contribution, 'Learning for Change?' documents the role that continuing educational opportunities can play in promoting participation and empowerment for people with learning difficulties and describes an innovative course to facilitate training by people with learning difficulties themselves. Dorothy Atkinson's chapter, 'Reclaiming our Past' meanwhile highlights the fundamental importance for people with learning difficulties of recovering knowledge about their own lives - knowledge which has so often been denied them in the past - with positive examples of empowerment through oral history and personal stories.

When self-advocacy (and citizen or third party advocacy) first developed in the UK, it was sometimes criticised as being a movement dominated by white, articulate men with only mild learning difficulties. **Section 4: Advocacy and Empowerment for All** demonstrates clearly that this is no longer the case. Each chapter in this Section focuses in turn on a different 'minority' group whose needs within the advocacy movement are, perhaps, only just beginning to be realised.

'Woman to Woman' describes, in the words of two self-advocates and their supporter, their experience of setting up and running a health advocacy group for women. Jackie Downer and Peter Ferns in their chapter explain why 'Self-Advocacy by Black People' is particularly important and how Black self-advocacy groups can work in practice. Traditionally advocacy has been seen as something for younger people. Jane Fitzgerald in her chapter, 'It's Never Too Late' presents some accounts of what empowerment can mean for older people with learning difficulties, based on a recent research project in this area. Similarly, advocacy has traditionally tended to exclude people with profound and multiple impairments. In 'A Say in My Future' Helen Sanderson describes clearly how people with profound and multiple impairments can be given voices and choices in their lives through person-centred planning. Finally in this Section, Ruth Marchant provides a powerful account of a self-advocacy group of disabled young people, many of whom do not communicate by speech, in her aptly entitled chapter 'Letting It Take Time'.

Advocacy and empowerment is about many things. It is about giving people voices and choices in their own lives. It is also about changing the policies and practices that have such a direct influence on the quality of life available to them. **Section 5**: **Changing Policies and Practices** provides five very different accounts of ways in which advocacy and involvement can bring about changes here.

In 'Who Chooses?' Margaret Macadam and Ruth Townsley describe an innovative project aimed at increasing the involvement of people with learning difficulties in the selection and recruitment of the staff who work with them and have such a big impact on their day to day lives. 'Choice and Control' is also about enabling people with learning difficulties to have more say in their daily lives. Here Andrew Holman and Jean Collins explain how recent legislation on direct payments can be made to work for people with learning difficulties, so that they can, if they choose, opt to receive cash instead of direct services from their local authority: money with which they can organise the kind of support and help that suits them best.

In 'Partners in Policymaking', Tara Barenok and Colleen Wieck look at another initiative designed to provide people with learning difficulties and their families with the skills that they need to help bring about changes in legislation, policies and practices in their area via the Partners in Policymaking programme which originated in the USA and has now been reproduced in other countries, including the UK.

The issue of how the law deals more generally with people with learning difficulties is the subject of Susan Hayes' chapter 'Justice for All?' She reviews the relative over-representation of people with learning difficulties within prisons and the many ways in which advocacy of all different kinds is required in order to ensure that people with learning difficulties get a fair deal from the justice system.

Finally, Ken Simons addresses the question: 'What really matters to people with learning difficulties?' by providing a wide range of positive examples of user involvement in changing policies and practice in his chapter 'Helping People with Learning Difficulties Change Services'.

Advocacy and Involvement for Children and Young People

It is no accident that most of the contributions to this volume centre on advocacy and empowerment for *adults* with learning difficulties. 'Listening' to disabled children, and acting on their wishes and concerns, is, on the whole, new territory in the UK.   Even where non-disabled children are concerned, we do not have a culture, on the whole, of listening to their views.   Child advocacy has, until recently, usually meant adults acting on their perceptions of the best interests of children, rather than representing the child's own view.   Supporting children and young people to speak up for themselves is much less common.

In any circumstances, advocacy involves addressing imbalances of power within our society and inevitably, raises dilemmas and difficulties.   But where children are concerned, particularly disabled children and young people, the risks of tokenism and exploitation are high and adult supporters have to pay special attention to how they address their role. As Ruth Marchant points out (Marchant, 1997) acting as an advocate as part of one's professional role can present real challenges and serious conflicts of interest.   Supporting a child's views and maintaining confidentiality, can create difficulties in terms of child protection, for example.   So it is vital that advocates, or professionals acting in an advocacy role, make it clear to children and young people with whom they are involved, just what the limitations of their role may be in terms of potential conflicts of interest with employers, the time and resources they have available, any limits to confidentiality and so on.

Both the Children Act 1989 and the UN Convention on the Rights of the Child embody key principles requiring that children - including disabled children - are consulted about decisions which affect their lives.   There is now a small, but growing, body of experience and literature on ways of doing this and of involving disabled children and young people in services and in research studies about them and their lives (Children and Society, 1996). At the Joseph Rowntree Foundation our expectation is that disabled children and young adults will be active participants in any project concerning them, though it is recognised that the involvement of some children, including those with profound and multiple impairments and those who do not communicate with speech or conventional signs, will pose particular challenges. Involving disabled children in projects means paying careful attention to safeguards and strategies, both to maximise their participation and to ensure their well-being. So a guide to resources, issues and strategies in this area has been produced (Ward, 1997b).

There are multiple issues and challenges to confront in this area. If we are serious about recognising disabled children and young people as appropriate respondents in research about their lives, then how do we go about ensuring meaningful consent? (See Alderson, 1995 for a detailed discussion on this.) What techniques can we use for work with disabled children who may not read or speak? (See Beresford, 1997 for a valuable review of the literature here). What kind of preparation is needed? What is an appropriate fee? What, in short, constitutes ethical involvement for disabled children in research or development projects? (Ward, 1997b).

We are also accumulating experience gradually in ways of involving disabled children and young people in the planning of projects and as advisers or consultants to them as they progress. Partnership can be important here. A group of disabled young people may know the issues they want to address and have relevant insights and contacts; building in specialised advice and support from others, where this is welcome, may strengthen their endeavour. Inevitably, both sceptics and supporters of involving disabled children alike worry about the possibility of bad experiences. But experience suggests that where young people complain of bad experiences of involvement it often centres on 'not knowing what's going on'. Early involvement, clear and accessible information, and proper preparation and training can make all the difference.

Involving People with Learning Difficulties in Research

Just as there has been a growing awareness of the need to listen to disabled children and involve them in projects which affect their lives, so too there has been increasing recognition that social research about things that matter to people with learning difficulties should, so far as possible and appropriate, involve them as partners in all the different stages of the research process. There have been enormous changes in this area over the last twenty years. In the 1970s research about people with learning difficulties did not involve them, even as respondents. The views of carers (staff or families) might be solicited instead.

But since the 1980s things have begun to change. More and more researchers are recognising that people with learning difficulties are the best respondents to comment on their experiences, aspirations and needs for support and that it is up to researchers to acquire and develop the innovative research skills which can make this possible. This is particularly necessary where the views of people with learning difficulties who may have only limited verbal communication skills or may communicate non-verbally are required.

Beyond that, there is now a clear expectation amongst some funding bodies (including the Joseph Rowntree Foundation) that research *about* disabled people should *involve* them in every possible stage and we now have positive models of practical ways in which people with learning difficulties can, and have been, involved as originators of research, as advisers or consultants to research projects, as research workers and interviewers and disseminators of research findings (see Ward, 1997a).

Margaret Macadam and Ruth Townsley's project at the Norah Fry Research Centre in Bristol, (described in Chapter 14) originated from a concern of people with learning difficulties locally about the very limited extent to which they were involved in the recruitment of staff in their homes and day centres. Although the research workers were non-disabled they were advised throughout by four panels of people with learning difficulties. They gave advice on the content and design of an accessible leaflet about the project, tested out materials for the pictorial interview schedule for people with learning difficulties in the study and gave their own experiences of involvement in staff recruitment to guide the researchers in formal interviews.

Over the last few years, there has been an increase too in the number of research projects which people with learning difficulties have undertaken themselves. In London, for example, People First - the organisation of people with learning difficulties - have carried out a study of the experiences of people with learning difficulties moving from long-stay institutions to homes in the community. The two interviewers from People First, with support from an adviser from Charities Evaluation Services, were trained to undertake the evaluation from carrying out the interviews right through to analysing and presenting the material in a report, in a summary and on tape (People First, 1994). Other examples of service evaluations by people with learning difficulties are given in *Looking at our Services* (Whittaker, 1997).

Elsewhere, people with learning difficulties are increasingly playing a crucial role as consultants and advisers. Indeed the Joseph Rowntree Foundation would now expect all research projects in this area which were not undertaken by people with learning difficulties themselves to demonstrate firm evidence of partnership with their organisations and their involvement as interviewers or consultants and advisers with appropriate payment of fees. What is more, there is an expectation that findings from the projects funded should be made available in an accessible format in ways which are useful to people with learning difficulties themselves. Hence the *Plain Facts* series described by Ruth Townsley in Chapter 5.

Clearly, most people with learning difficulties - like their non-disabled peers - will have no great desire to carry out research themselves. But recent experience is showing that, for those who do, appropriate support can ensure that participation in research in whatever way can be an empowering experience.

Research that we do ourselves will make sure that we are in control. Most research has not consulted us fully and we have been researched on by professionals when we are the experts. We have decided what to find out and we will lead it. We will make sure that other people with disabilities know what we have found out. By doing it this way we will learn a lot ourselves. We will help make sure that in future we are fully consulted. (React, 1996)

Looking to the Future

This chapter started with some snapshots of exciting examples of advocacy and empowerment for people with learning difficulties. As this volume makes clear, all over the country and indeed the world further positive and inspiring examples abound. People with learning difficulties alone or together, with the support of non-disabled allies or their disabled peers are making their views, wishes and voices heard and, where things are working well, changes are taking place. They are carrying out research, they are advising service purchasers and providers. They are training themselves, other people with learning difficulties and the professionals who work with them. They are commenting on plans, complaining about initiatives with which they do not agree, organising and speaking at conferences and indeed, in the case of Barb Goode, addressing the United Nations itself (See Foreword). This is the public face of advocacy and empowerment and involvement in action.

And for every one of these high profile activities, there are many more examples of people with learning difficulties, their non-disabled allies, families and members of their local community coming together for change. This book is a celebration of all these initiatives and an encouragement to us all to do more and to do better in the future.

A note on terminology

The terminology adopted within the title of this book is 'people with intellectual disabilities' because that is the internationally recognised term adopted by the World Health Organisation. Within different countries, other terms may be preferred. In the UK, for example, 'people with learning difficulties' is the term most often used, by people who bear that label themselves. It is, therefore, used widely by UK contributors to this book. 'People with learning disabilities' is another term widely accepted in the UK not least by the Department of Health. That term is also to be found within this volume.

Terminology which is now considered negative and stigmatising, for example 'mental handicap' 'mentally retarded' and so on is used within the chapters that follow only where is it historically appropriate or to indicate issues about negative labelling of this kind.

Within the UK at least, there is now increasing awareness of the importance of the 'social model of disability'. Within the social model of disability the actual impairment (physical, intellectual or sensory) experienced by individuals is less important than the disabling barriers and attitudes created and sustained by the society in which they live - for example, the presentation of material in non-accessible formats, inaccessible public transport and buildings and so on. Those adopting the social model of disability will tend to refer to disabled people as 'disabled people', rather than as 'people with disabilities', on the grounds that they are in fact disabled by the society in which they live. This terminology too is to be found within the chapters that follow.

Acknowledgments

My thanks to Ruth Marchant for her helpful comments in relation to advocacy and children. Thanks also to Angela Martin for the illustration used in this chapter.

References

Alderson, P. (1995) *Listening to Children: Children, Ethics and Social Research*. Barkingside: Barnardo's.

Beresford, B. (1997) *Personal Accounts: Involving Disabled Children in Research*. London: The Stationery Office.

Children and Society (1996) 10, No. 2 (Issue focussing on the ethics and methodology of research with children).

Knight, A. (1998a) Independent Visitors and Disabled Young People, *Findings,* No. 138, January. York: Joseph Rowntree Foundation.

Knight, A. (1998b) *Valued or Forgotten? Disabled Children and Independent   Visitors*. London: National Children's Bureau.

Marchant, R. (1997) *Personal Communication*.

Mental Health Foundation (1996) *Building expectations: opportunities and services for people with a learning disability*. London: Mental Health Foundation.

People First (1994) *Outside but not inside ...yet?* London: People First.

React (1996) Funding proposal to the Joseph Rowntree Foundation. Preston: Youth Research Action on Learning Disability.

Ward L. (1997a) Funding for change: translating emancipatory disability research from theory to practice. In Barnes, C. and Mercer, D. (eds.) *Doing Disability Research*. Leeds: The Disability Press.

Ward, L. (1997b) *Seen & Heard: Involving Disabled Children and Young People in Research and Development Projects*. York: York Publishing.

Whittaker, A. (1997) *Looking at our Services: Service evaluation by people with learning difficulties*. London: King's Fund.

Linda Ward is Programme Adviser (Disability) to the Joseph Rowntree Foundation (the UK's largest independent funder of research and development projects in the fields of housing, social policy, disability and social care) where she has particular responsibility for work on disabled children and young people and on independent living and direct payments for disabled people.

She is also Senior Research Fellow at the University of Bristol's Norah Fry Research Centre where she has researched and written widely on learning difficulties and disability and is currently Social Research Adviser to the National Lottery Charities Board on their health and social research grants programme. She has a strong interest in equal opportunities issues and has been involved in different capacities in the advocacy field for many years.

Contact address

Norah Fry Research Centre
University of Bristol
3 Priory Road
BRISTOL BS8 1TX
England

Section 2

Coming Together for Change

2 One Day at a Time
Changing a System to Realise a Dream

Ray Browning, John O'Brien and Connie Lyle O'Brien

Ray is one of the pioneers in our home state of Georgia who have worked with their allies to change the way services are delivered. They prove beyond doubt that people with severe disabilities can live safely, and usually comfortably, in their own homes, with assistance from agencies and staff that they can hire and fire.

After fourteen years as a 'heavy care' patient in a nursing home with more than 100 other disabled and elderly people, Ray moved into his own place. Every day for more than two years, Ray has shown that people who need a lot of assistance with everyday matters - like getting dressed and eating; using the toilet and getting from place to place; reading and writing - that they don't have to live in institutions or nursing homes or group homes or staff supervised apartments. Like anyone else, they can live in their own homes if they have adequate assistance.

There have been many problems to solve and some hard times, and there will be many more difficulties. But those problems, and labels like 'severe cerebral palsy' and 'uncorrectable vision deficits' and 'moderate mental retardation', don't have to determine where you live, who you live with, how you spend your day, and how you get the help you need.

Ray has helped to change the rules in our state's service system and to make the world of possibilities bigger for a growing number of people with disabilities. Along the way he has learned a lot about how to play a part in making social change. It is very important to him to teach other people what he has learned. He has talked about his journey out of the nursing home to people with disabilities and their families, to politicians and service managers, to staff, and to people in his community.

Connie and John have become Ray's friends and allies. One of the things they help Ray to do is to tell his story; that is their task in writing this chapter with him. The story is Ray's and the chapter will include three of his papers. The lessons about change come mostly from John and Connie's reflections on Ray's story which Ray has reviewed and approved.

Ray lives in the United States but we think lessons from his experience can help anyone who wants to work for change in a system that segregates people with disabilities and takes away their choices about where to live and how to organise the help they need. Where we live in Georgia, nursing homes are the most common services that separate disabled people from the community and control their lives. In other places, separation and control happen in institutions, hostels, group homes or even in supported living services. The details of the system's rules are different from place to place, but we think that there are many similarities in what it takes to make systems fit better to the kind of lives people want to live.

Why and How Does Ray Write?

Ray takes time to make up his mind about things. His first answer to a question is usually very short, and is far from including everything that he thinks or feels about a subject. He thinks hard and carefully about what he wants for himself and for other people with disabilities. His ideas come to him a bit at a time. Ray does not read or write, so he likes to have someone he trusts to act as his scribe, writing down his ideas as they come to him and then helping him to organise them. When he has an idea, he will often call on the telephone and dictate a note, or ask someone nearby to write down the idea in his notebook. Once he has a number of ideas, he likes to have them typed on a computer and read back to him, because that makes it easy for him to rearrange the order of his thoughts and choose just the words he wants. When a paper suits him, he usually takes multiple copies of the final version and shares them widely. Connie has been Ray's scribe more often than anyone else.

Ray usually writes in order to work for change. He has written testimony for public hearings about services to people with disabilities, letters to politicians, and talks for conferences. Because it can be difficult for people to understand his speech, he usually asks someone else to read his papers for him and then he answers questions.

Sometimes, Ray wants to write about a question so he can understand something better for himself. He has dictated several notes for himself about difficulties he has in effectively directing his personal assistants, especially his paid roommates.

Two Kinds of Change

From time to time, people decide to change their living arrangements. They move to a larger or smaller place, or move in with someone, or move out to be on their own. People with disabilities who need everyday assistance provided by a service system often find these moves hard to make. Too often, the service system decides where a person will live and with whom; when a person will move and even what kind of furniture they will have. Usually these decisions are based on professional assessments, though it is hard to see why professional skill entitles control of someone's living arrangements.

Rules make service systems: rules about who makes decisions and how decisions are made; rules about how money can be spent and who can spend it; rules about what kinds of assistance are allowed and how much assistance will be available. These rules are written down in laws, regulations, policies, plans, budgets and protocols, and system workers produce documentation that proves that they are following them. Behind the rules there are beliefs about how life can and should be for people with disabilities; some of these beliefs are written down, but most of them are taken for granted. The beliefs behind the rules may be so powerful that people in the system take them as the way things are and have to be. People reckon, 'that's just reality'.

Change within the Rules

Sometimes a person wants a change that the service system can assist with if it's within its current rules and beliefs. The person may have to wait for necessary assistance to become available, or to argue a case with officials, or to lobby for more funds for the service system, but people in the system can do what needs to be done by following the rules. Problems have to do with resources: having money enough, or properly qualified staff enough, or space enough to do what's needed.

Sometimes a change that makes sense for a person isn't possible within the system's present rules and beliefs. Often people shorten this sentence and simply say, 'That change isn't possible'. When they forget that the system works through actions that follow changeable rules and beliefs, they shrink the world of opportunities. When they stop even wondering about possibilities outside the system's rules and beliefs, the world of opportunities shrinks even more because people's ideas about a desirable future shrivel to fit what the system offers.

Changing the Rules

There is a chance to make the world of opportunities bigger whenever a group of people takes the courage to ask: 'Why isn't this sensible change possible? What would it take to make it happen?' There is only a chance of positive change, not a certainty, because many people hold on to the rules and beliefs that make the system. Even if they don't like the way it works, the system provides them or someone they love with assistance, or it provides them with a job and an income and a career. Perhaps some of its buildings or routines or accomplishments give them a feeling of satisfaction and familiarity that they would be fearful or sad to lose. As long as people stay inside the beliefs that make the system, they cannot imagine changing it when it frustrates and angers them by ruling out possibilities that make sense, or even when it dominates their lives.

A Crack Opens in the System

Seven years ago in Georgia, system rules didn't allow people with disabilities to get more than a few hours of paid assistance a day in their own homes, and the kinds of tasks that assistants could do were very tightly defined in medical terms. Most people with severe disabilities either lived with their families or in a nursing home.

Seven years ago, Ray was in his ninth year of living in a nursing home. Because his mother couldn't physically assist him anymore, he knew his family had done all they could and that there was nowhere else for him to go. The nursing home was all there was to 'reality' for him and everyone he knew. Ray made the best of it. His family had found a good nursing home near their homes and visited him. He went out to church and on whatever outings the nursing home organised. He kept busy.

Seven years ago a small group of disabled activists and a few of their allies created a small window of opportunity to shift the system's rules. Two disabled organisers had created ways to make their living that allowed them to bring people together to work on breaking the nursing home's monopoly on 'reality' for people with severe disabilities. This meant learning how the political system worked: who to lobby, how to pressure, when to try to influence the process of law making, budgeting and planning. It meant staying coordinated with other activists working to open up jobs, housing, heath care and public transportation to disabled people. It meant learning the system's rules so well that they know them better than most people who work full time managing the system. So when technical changes in laws and funding rules made more flexibility possible, a small and determined group of people were ready to push the system into a new shape. The organisers' names are Pat Puckett and Mark Johnson. Without their willingness to challenge other people with disabilities to organise themselves, and their skill at learning how to push from outside the system on the details of the way the system works, Ray would still be making the best of the nursing home.

This small but growing network of activists pushed the question, 'If the system will pay for someone to live in a nursing home, why won't it pay for the personal assistance people require to live in their own homes?' They asked this question, and presented their own proposals for system change, over and over and over. And mostly, the people they talked with couldn't hear them, because they were speaking from outside what people took as 'reality': most people just knew that people with severe disabilities belong in nursing homes. These change-agents got used to having conversations about a system based on new beliefs with people who treated them like peculiar visitors from the planet Pluto. And, after two persistent years, a few people inside the system heard enough of the message to create the possibility for the first person in our state to try a new way to live her life her way. Because she needs assistance with every activity – including assuring that her ventilator continues to breathe for her – her widely publicised ability to live well in her own home disproved the need for nursing homes and showed how a change in system rules could make a positive difference. Her name is Jenny Langley, and her personal and political activism opened a tiny crack in Georgia's institutional 'reality'. Within a year, a pilot program assisted 30 people to live in their own places. This is the crack in the system that grew wide enough to allow Ray the choice to roll free from his nursing home.

Ray Gets Involved

Part of the strategy for making bigger the first tiny crack in institutional 'reality' was to document what the change meant for people with severe disabilities. Connie helped a group of people with disabilities and family members to study the system and define new beliefs and new rules based on their experience and desires (Lyle O'Brien, 1992). Because the separation of people with disabilities into separate groups is one of the ways the system maintains control over people's thinking and their lives, the study included some people with physical disabilities and some people with developmental disabilities (the system category that includes most people with learning disabilities, cerebral palsy and autism in our state).

This decision brought Ray's friend Fred Pinson into the study. Fred, Ray and Cecil (another man with cerebral palsy) met in the nursing home and supported each other to deal with the problems of living there. Fred had thought about moving out before, but he and his citizen advocates kept running up against the system rules that made it impossible for him to get the amount and kind of assistance he requires outside of a nursing home. The chance that the system's rules could change revived Fred's interest.

He asked Connie and John to join a number of other people in his support circle and they agreed.

One day, Connie, Fred and Cecil were in the nursing home's dining room talking about what it would take for Fred to move into his own home. Ray rolled up and asked what they were talking about. Cecil said: 'We're planning a way to escape from here. Do you want to come?' Ray said: 'No. But I do need a new TV in my room.' Then he asked Connie: 'Will you get me a TV?' Connie explained that she was there to help Fred and Cecil figure out how to get out. She did offer to give Ray a ride to check the prices on TVs in several stores.

On the trip to shop for a TV, Ray talked to Connie about getting out of the nursing home. Over the next few weeks, Ray took action to expand his world of possibilities. He asked Fred and Connie lots of questions. He met Jenny Langley and asked her questions about how she organised her personal assistance system. He attended a conference with Fred, Cecil and Connie, where he met Michael Callahan, a leader in developing supported employment for people with multiple disabilities, and learned that, in other states, people with disabilities similar to his were getting the assistance they needed to work in ordinary jobs. He joined in the first meeting of Fred's circle of support and helped Fred make his personal futures plan. He attended a meeting of SAN, the advocacy network organised to change the system and decided to join. He learned that the system was holding public hearings about its plans, and that SAN was encouraging people to testify about the need for change.

After gathering new ideas, Ray thought hard about his own dreams and desires for himself, and he decided he wanted to recruit a circle of support and move out. He asked John to help him make a personal plan for the move.

Ray decided that the decision makers needed to know about his plan, so he testified at the hearing about the medical assistance plan. This is what he said (July-August 1993, Testimony to Georgia Department of Medical Assistance Hearings):

My name is Ray Browning and I am 35 years old. I have to live in a nursing home and I don't want to. I want out of the nursing home. I want my own place to live and a real job so I can help pay for what I need. I have cerebral palsy but I'm not sick. I do need help to get in and out of bed, in and out of a car, with my bath, dressing, buying groceries, cooking, going to the bathroom. I need someone to help me with my money. I want a lift-equipped van and someone to drive it for me. I need a way to get to the places I need to go, when I need to go there; like to go to work, to Mt. Zion, my church, and to see my family and friends.

Families need help too. My family took care of me as long as they could. They did not want to put me in a nursing home. Before they did, they looked for help to come to my house, but they couldn't find any. They don't want me in the nursing home, but they can't take care of me without help. My family loves me. They still do lots of things for me now. My mother does my laundry every week, and my brother stops by to fix my wheelchair when it breaks. My father visits me once a week and my uncle cuts my hair. I talk to my mother and my father every day on the telephone. They've done everything they can for me including taking care of me until they couldn't do it anymore. I don't understand why families can't get help at home when they need it.

I don't understand why the government will pay money to keep me in a nursing home and won't pay money to help me get my own place to live with the help I need to live there. I don't understand why the government can't help me get a job so I can pay for some of the things I need.

I don't know how much money the nursing home gets to keep me, but I only get $30.00 a month. In the nursing home I sometimes have to wait for an hour for someone to help me go to the bathroom, and sometimes I have to sit on the toilet for an hour where someone has left me and has not come back for an hour even though I turn the light on. I can't sleep at night because there are two other men in the *room who make noise or keep their lights on. There is no place where I can have privacy. There are always people coming in and out or walking around. My things go missing. I see other people wearing my clothes. I don't want a better nursing home. I want my own place and the help I need to live there.*

I am learning about some new programs in Georgia. There is one called the Independent Care Waiver[1] that offers personal assistance services which is what I need, but there is not enough money for all the people who need it. I have been told there is no more money for this waiver to support other people until April 1994. There should be more money for things like this to help me live in my own place. There should be money to help families so they don't have to put me in a nursing home.

Ray's family couldn't understand what he was saying about wanting to live in his own place. While their sense of opportunities stayed inside the nursing home, his was expanding rapidly beyond it. His mother worried that people were misleading or even using Ray, because she knew it was unrealistic to think about living outside a nursing home. She was afraid that Ray might anger the nursing home owner and lose his place there. Without the nursing home, she would have no choice but to try and care for him. Ray asked his mother and father to take some time to find out about what was possible. He told them that he wanted and needed their support but that he would make up his own mind about where to live. Ray's parents have always respected his right to choose, and they agreed to help as much as they could.

---

1 A 'waiver' is a way the system suspends some of its rules to allow its workers to do something different. Waivers have their own written rules and monitoring procedures that define exactly how the system will behave when it assists someone under the waiver. The Independent Care Waiver allowed a few people great flexibility in the use of system money according to an individual plan and budget prepared by the person and their allies but reviewed and approved and closely monitored by the system.

Making the Long Haul

Changing the beliefs and rules that create a system takes a lot of work and can take a long time. For Ray, it took more than two years to get from his first plan to his first lease on an apartment of his own. His motto for these years was: 'We'll get there, but we have to take it one day at a time'.

Ray didn't wait for the system to change, he worked to change it. SAN (the self-advocacy group) and the Disability Rights Center had some money to pay for transportation and personal assistants for members involved in influencing the system and educating themselves. Ray used these funds to attend meetings and conferences. He spoke up about the importance of change every time he had the chance. He lobbied politicians, participated in system planning groups, and talked to his church about getting people out of nursing homes.

Whenever Ray met someone he thought could help him change the system, he asked for their help. This is the paper he gave people to explain his request (February 1995):

The most important thing I need in order to get out of the nursing home is money from the Independent Care Waiver Program, which is administered by the Georgia Department of Medical Assistance (DMA).

You can help me get a place in the Independent Care Waiver in three ways:

- *Give me rides to and from meetings that will help me get a waiver and take notes for me. Meetings like Self-Advocacy Network (SAN) meetings and DMA and DHR (Department of Human Resources) hearings.*

- *Write letters or call the Governor's office, DMA, and legislators and tell them to put more money into the Independent Care Waiver. Tell them that Ray Browning needs it to get out of the nursing home.*

- *Give me other ideas or help me meet people you think can help me.*

I want people to join my circle of support to help me figure out what to do and how to do it. So far, the whole circle meets every month or two and members work on other things with me in between meetings. When I get my waiver, the circle will get more active in helping me set up my home.

When I get a place in the Independent Care Waiver Program I will need:

- *People who I can hire to be my personal assistants. I need very reliable people who will be willing to learn what I need and how I want things done.*

- *Information on housing in Gwinnett County that is accessible and affordable.*

If you want to help me, please write your name, address, and phone number(s) here so I can put it in my book.

Ray has a gift for asking. He is gracious when people help and when they say no or disagree. He is not discouraged when people say no to his requests.

More than 100 people signed up to help Ray and many of them did. Some people helped in small ways by offering suggestions and encouragement, writing a letter to their representative, contributing to Ray's van fund, or suggesting another person to contact or another meeting to attend. People gave him rides or helped him arrange rides. Two of the nursing home staff accepted Ray's invitation to provide personal assistance when he went to a meeting or conference, liked working for him, and agreed to work for him when he moved out. Some people offered Ray furnishings for his home. Other people helped Ray do things he wanted to outside the nursing home, like attending a literacy program at the public library. Some system managers say that Ray's forthright and thoughtful explanations of why he wanted to move out and why he did not want to live in a small group home and his direct request that they do what they could to assist him, helped them to expand their own beliefs about what their system could and should support.

Ray took responsibility for coordinating action on his own behalf. He has a very good sense of planning and a good memory for what people have committed to do. He can use a touch pad phone if a number is written down and he can remember many telephone numbers. A supply of coins to operate the nursing home pay phone from circle members made it possible for Ray to track and organise their activity and his involvement in the work for system change. Anyone who promised to help out got accustomed to reminder and follow-up calls from Ray.

Ray's beliefs are generally conservative. He thought very hard about whether or not he would get involved in political demonstrations and civil disobedience organised by disabled activists to raise the issues of creating alternatives to the segregation and professional control of people with disabilities. In the end, he decided that he would participate in direct action to change the system, even if it meant that he would risk getting arrested.

Ray worked hard to make change, and sometimes it seemed like he would never get out of the nursing home. This is Ray's list of things that kept him going (June 1995):

- *Having people to listen to me who know that I can think and do not laugh or get scared when I say what my dreams are and what I want.*

- *Having a circle and a plan so a lot of people can each do a little bit and the little bits fit together.*

- *Being part of Fred's circle and helping Fred get out.*

- *Being part of SAN and the Disability Rights Center. Getting involved in politics and testifying at hearings. It helps to keep telling different people what has to change and why it's important. It helps to know you're part of a movement.*

- *Speaking to groups about people having their own homes and listening for new ideas.*

- *Finding out about how other people with disabilities live and work and how they set up their personal assistance system.*

- *Keeping my book of people and ideas.*

- *Going to conferences, especially about rights, jobs, and homes.*

- *Fighting to make the nursing home a better place to live while we had to be here (even though it didn't even really work). Getting out of the nursing home as much as possible[2].*

In August 1995, a place in the Independent Care funding stream became available unexpectedly and Ray moved at short notice into his own apartment. His personal assistants and his roommate were people he had recruited himself. His housewarming party brought many of the people who had supported him together to celebrate. He also invited several people with disabilities he had met through SAN. They had not yet decided whether to seek their way out of nursing homes. Ray wanted them to see what is possible when people work together to move outside the system's usual rules and beliefs.

Some Lessons for Organisers

- The more widely and strongly people hold system-shaping beliefs as defining the limits of reality, the more important it is to build a base for change outside the system. A small group must support one another to define and pursue possibilities which challenge the system's beliefs and strengthen the case for new rules.

---

2   The nursing home took a neutral position on Ray's work to make change. They allowed visits and meetings with no hassles for most of the time Ray was working to get out and did not interfere with Ray coming and going.

- The more skill and energy organisers can devote to building the base group, the faster and more widely the movement for change can grow. Full-time organisers seldom have much in the way of income or job security; some organisers use their benefits income to fund their social change work and can extend their effectiveness greatly if they can find help with telephone, copying, faxing, mailing and transport expenses.

- To change the system, some people in the base group need to learn the political processes for changing the system's rules by getting directly involved (don't forget work for political parties).

- Some people need to learn the details of the system's rules and workings very well, while not mistaking them for unchangeable reality. The goal is to understand what the rules already allow that's *not* being done and to identify exactly the rules that must change if things are to be different.

- Find a question that challenges the beliefs that shape the system's rules and keep asking it to anyone with power in the system.

- The base group needs to have an answer to its question, but getting people wondering about the question is more important at first than getting them to accept your answer. Once people accept the question, they usually have good ideas on improving the answer.

- Don't expect people to even understand the question at first. Remember, it may come from outside their sense of what reality is.

- As soon as possible, use some system resources to create the difference you want to make in the life of at least one person. A system insider who believes in a new possibility can free resources in the name of a pilot project or an experiment or a response to political pressure. Inventing a new way of being takes courage, creative problem solving, negotiating skill, and willingness to work hard. All these skills can be developed by actually making the change.

- Even though the existence of a new way to live disproves the beliefs that shape the system, expect most people to dismiss it as a weird exception instead of changing their beliefs. But, at least a few other people will now be able to see expanded possibilities and join or support the base group.

- Sometimes small amounts of system money can be found to support studies, evaluations, plans, and consultation exercises that explore the base group's change question. Do a good job of meeting the system's needs for information and ideas in a way that puts people with disabilities in charge and brings people with disabilities together to explore their experience in terms of the base group's question. The studies and plans won't change the system, but they can expand the base group, clarify thinking, and support problem solving. Budgets for this kind of work need to allow for the expenses of transportation, communication, and personal assistance required by people with disabilities.

- When you take system money, deliver what you promised, on time and in an attractive form. Most people inside the system won't be persuaded by documents and presentations, but keeping agreements protects credibility.

- Work across a wide spectrum of approaches to change, from joining system working groups to civil disobedience. Keep asking how involvement in system activities like planning exercises and providing representation on committees helps move change forward and pull back to minimal involvement when there is not much promise of change.

- Always keep a human face on the issues.

- Always look for what the next new person with a disability can contribute to changing the system.

Acknowledgements

Preparation of this paper was partially supported through a subcontract to Responsive Systems Associates from the Center on Human Policy, Syracuse University for the Research and Training Center on Community

Living. The Research and Training Center on Community Living is supported through a cooperative agreement (number H133B30072) between the National Institute on Disability & Rehabilitation Research (NIDRR) and the University of Minnesota Institute on Community Integration. Members of the Center are encouraged to express their opinions; these do not necessarily represent the official position of NIDRR.

Reference

Lyle O'Brien, C. (1992) *To Boldly Go...* Atlanta, Georgia:
Georgia Governor's Council on Developmental Disabilities.

Ray Browning works to help people with disabilities keep out and move out of nursing homes and institutions. He lives in his own home in Snellville, Georgia.

John O'Brien and Connie Lyle O'Brien learn about building more just and inclusive communities from people with disabilities, their families, and their allies. They use what they learn to advise people with disabilities and their families, advocacy groups, service providers, and governments and to spread the news among people interested in change by writing and through workshops. They are members of the Center on Human Policy at Syracuse University.

Contact address

Responsive Systems Associates
58 Willowick Drive
Lithonia
Georgia 30038 - 1722
U.S.A.

3 Self-Advocacy
Speaking Up for Ourselves and Each Other
Bridget Whittell, Paul Ramcharan and Members of People First Cardiff and the Vale

When I started in a self-advocacy group, it helped me quite a lot, learning to speak out...

...we help others with learning disabilities.

Introduction

This chapter has been written in co-operation with the members of a county-wide self-advocacy forum based in Cardiff. A visit was made to meet and talk with members and the discussion was taped. After this was transcribed, a draft of the chapter was written and sent to the group - together with a version on audio tape - so they could check it to make sure they were happy with how it sounded. This is important because self-advocacy is about people speaking up for themselves. Writing or finding out about self-advocacy should be done with or by the people who are directly involved.

In 1994, members of People First Wales decided to find out what was happening with different self-advocacy groups in Wales. Questionnaires were circulated to all 58 self-advocacy groups known to exist at that time and these were completed and returned by 46 groups. Some of the findings from this survey (Ramcharan et al.,1996) are reflected in this chapter, along with the views of members of People First Cardiff and the Vale. Members talk about what self-advocacy means to them and why it is important. They also discuss some of their struggles and achievements, and their aims and hopes for the future.

Although this chapter is based on the views and experiences of people involved in self-advocacy in Wales, it covers issues which may be more widely relevant to self-advocacy and people with learning disabilities. Members of People First Cardiff and the Vale represent the views of people with learning disabilities in different settings - community based, hospital based, day centre based and community education based. They have some clear messages about what makes self-advocacy work and what sort of help and support is needed for self-advocacy to continue to develop and flourish into the next millennium.

Who We Are and What We Are Doing

A group of people sticking together, and discussing things, and speaking up for yourself.

How self-advocacy groups start and develop, and how members see themselves and what they are doing is a part of their identity.   In Cardiff, there is a strong link between self-advocacy and community adult education.   When the first seven groups were set up in 1989 it was decided that they should meet in community locations such as adult education centres. Facilitators to help support the groups were trained by the South Glamorgan Institute of Higher Education.   However, some self-advocacy groups were also started in day centres and other service settings, and by 1992 there were eleven groups in Cardiff and the Vale based in community education and seven groups linked to social services.

Since 1994 the community education self-advocacy groups have been funded via local colleges by the Further Education Funding Council for Wales. The growth and development of self-advocacy in the Cardiff area has also been helped by funding made available under the All Wales Strategy (Welsh Office, 1983).   Indeed, the People First Wales survey in 1994 showed that All Wales Strategy funding played a crucial role in helping the development of self-advocacy for people with learning disabilities throughout Wales.

PEOPLE FIRST
CARDIFF AND THE VALE

WORKING TO MAKE PEOPLE UNDERSTAND
WHAT WE ALL WANT OUT OF LIFE

Despite the various self-advocacy groups from which members of People First Cardiff and the Vale come, they have a strong sense of being part of a single, common group. They enjoy going and belonging to a self-advocacy group: 'I like it. It's good.' They have status. They are respected. People are proud of who they are, what they are doing and of belonging to a group with a strong identity. This is reinforced by people having membership cards and a common logo; they produce their own newsletter and sell tee-shirts, sweatshirts, keyrings, mugs and pens, all bearing their name and distinctive logo. Promotional products help to raise the profile of People First Cardiff and the Vale and are also a way of increasing funds.

Identity and ownership is also seen in what members do. For example, the members of one self-advocacy group changed the name: 'It was called self-advocacy, but it was such a mouthful that my friends and myself decided to change it to something which was easier.' And another group decided to finish '... because it was becoming too much of a social group, and we didn't want that, and it wasn't fulfilling the proper purpose....' This also shows the ongoing and developing nature of self-advocacy, especially as members take more control for themselves.

As some groups finish, others start up, but all the while self-advocacy is growing and strengthening and getting more people involved. In 1989 the seven groups in the Cardiff area had a membership of 87 people. Since then this figure has more than doubled. Around 200 people are now involved in self-advocacy groups in Cardiff and the Vale, with 20 groups based in community education and social service settings such as day centres and Ely Hospital. The People First Cardiff and the Vale Committee comprises representatives from all the different self-advocacy groups in Cardiff and the Vale and they meet in a community setting: a room in a local leisure centre.

People join and get involved with self-advocacy in a variety of ways. The relatively large number of groups in the Cardiff area also gives people a choice. One woman stopped going to a group because she found it was too loud and noisy, but was able to join another group that met on a different night that suited her better 'because it was a bit more quiet.' The close links between self-advocacy and community education in the Cardiff area means that many people can choose, or are invited, to join a self-advocacy 'class'. People should know they have a choice where this is possible. Unfortunately, in some areas in Britain where self-advocacy is still not well developed, or where people would have to travel too far to join a different self-advocacy group, this is still not possible.

Good Practice Point:
Having a choice of more than one self-advocacy group to join can be important. People should be facilitated to join a group where they feel comfortable, valued and respected.

Self-advocacy: What it is and What We are Doing

Self-advocacy – we talk about making choices, sticking up for ourselves.

Self-advocacy – a meeting place to learn ideas… we speak about different things.

A commonly shared view amongst members of People First Cardiff and the Vale was that self-advocacy was about speaking up, and learning to speak up, both for themselves and other people.   Perhaps not surprisingly, those belonging to self-advocacy groups based within service settings tended to express a view about self-advocacy that reflects an interest in local service issues and problems connected to where their group is located:

We talk about things to do with the Centre like vandalism and a recent fire, outings, operational policy, planning…

Residents' Committee. We're speaking up for residents' rights and for people who can't speak for themselves…

However, talking and listening to people from different groups also indicated a shared sense and understanding of self-advocacy that was much wider, extending beyond their rights as 'service users' to their rights as 'citizens', such as their right to get a job. People saw self-advocacy as: 'telling people about their rights… that they have equal rights, human rights…' and speaking out against unfair treatment and discrimination, such as being labelled: 'I prefer the term learning difficulty or learning disability. I was labelled myself years ago as mentally defective… but we are not mentally defective just because we are disabled… disability is not inability…'

Belonging to a self-advocacy group was also seen as being about friendship, and caring about each other:

I go because it's a friendly atmosphere, and it's more like a family to me...

I go to talk to people... and meeting friends as well...

> *We're a caring group. If there's a bereavement, we send flowers, and if there's somebody ill, we send a get well card... we're like a family, if something happens to somebody, we know about it.*

> *Some people share their problems with us and tell us, and we try to do something about it if we can... we're a good shoulder for people to cry on.*

There was also agreement that as well as self-advocacy being about talking to people and 'speaking up', it was also about listening and offering advice:

> *I would say advocacy is being a good listener as well, listening to people and their problems... It's being a good listener... Sometimes in advocacy, it's like being a doctor, you have got to be a good doctor and know what prescription to give, what advice to give...*

However, at the same time, it was realised that there were limitations to what self-advocacy could do: '...some people think we can wave a magic wand, but we can't...'

Good Practice Point:
The views of members about the meaning and purpose of self-advocacy are very important. Sharing views gives a common identity and purpose. Being in control of these and talking about them also allows members to tell whether they are developing as a group, i.e. 'doing' as well as 'talking', which is regarded as an essential progression step for self-advocacy (for example, see Whittaker, 1991).

Activities and Achievements

Members of People First Cardiff and the Vale have been involved in a lot of 'doing' work as well as 'talking'. One person described self-advocacy as being 'a job to learn... the more you learn about self-advocacy, the more you get interested...' As people get more interested, they get more involved and active. Belonging to a self-advocacy group has collective and individual benefits for people. At a collective level, the voice of people with learning disabilities is being heard, listened to and taken seriously in many places and their representation on various groups and committees is now well established. Learning how to speak up and belonging to a self-advocacy group also gives individuals more confidence: 'Since being in self-advocacy, I've come out a lot.' 'Since talking to people, I feel more confident. When I first started, I felt nervous.' However, learning to speak up confidently is only a part of being involved in self-advocacy.

Some of the achievements and the different activities which members of People First Cardiff and the Vale are involved in include:

- Speaking up about their rights and telling other people about their rights. For example, making people aware of complaints procedures.

- Helping people to speak up for themselves and helping and supporting people to make choices and decisions.

- Training and talking to other people about self-advocacy and issues concerning people with learning disabilities. For example, two members are involved with training student nurses, and members help to train people who want to get involved in supporting self-advocacy groups.

- Making information more accessible. Members have highlighted the difficulties that they have in reading and understanding many documents. The Residents' Group of Ely Hospital have helped to make the Residents' Charter more accessible by putting it onto audio tape. Minutes of self-advocacy meetings are also put on to audio tape.

- Helping to make changes to improve people's lives. This includes things like improving access. Members have successfully campaigned to get a lift installed in one of the community adult education buildings and a stair rail installed in another. People First Cardiff and the Vale were also asked to help SCOPE (the cerebral palsy organisation) in a survey looking at accessibility for disabled voters.

People First, Cardiff and The Vale

Wider Representation & Membership

* Cardiff Joint Commissioning Group
* Standing Conference of Voluntary Organisations (S.C.O.V.O.)

* Cardiff Consultation Group
* Voluntary Action Cardiff

* Vale Advisory Planning Group
* Vale Council for Voluntary Services

* Cardiff County Council Equal Opportunities Sub-Committee Disability Advisory Group
* Cardiff and Vale Coalition of Disabled People

* People First Wales

Committee composed of representatives from:

Self-Advocacy Groups in Cardiff and the Vale
Day Services in Cardiff and the Vale
Ely's People First – Ely Hospital
(Links with Opportunity Housing Trust Tenants' Action Group)

Activities

* issues
* newsletter
* information
* conferences
* minutes
* consultation

With and for

* **Service users**
* **Self-advocacy groups**
* **Ely Hospital residents**

- Representing the views of people with learning disabilities on a number of committees and groups in the voluntary and statutory sector (see Figure; p.46).

Good Practice Point:
Widening representation and continuing to recruit are important aspects of the work and role of self-advocacy groups.

- Working to improve the quality of services. For example, the Residents' Group at Ely Hospital were successful in getting a menu system introduced so that people had a choice of food, and in reinstating the availability of snacks on the wards.

- Planning and organising their own annual People First conference and attending other self-advocacy conferences.

- Producing their own self-advocacy newsletter up to three times a year which is distributed to members and other interested people.

- People have also found the confidence to speak up about bad things that were happening to them, such as abuse or exploitation. For example, one group helped to expose abuse that had been taking place at one of the day centres. The group held their meetings in a community setting and were supported by a facilitator who did not work for social services.

Good Practice Point:
Self-advocacy groups being supported by someone independent of the services people receive is seen as important by many people involved in self-advocacy. Holding meetings in a neutral, community setting also encourages people to feel more relaxed and speak up more freely and openly. Another advantage of meeting in a community setting is that people get to meet and talk to other people, apart from service staff and people with learning disabilities.

Making Self-Advocacy Work

Becoming more independent was mentioned as one of the things that helped to make self-advocacy work, but there are many other things as well. Members of People First Cardiff and the Vale gave some clear messages about what they felt was needed to make self-advocacy work and what helped to make it successful.

Learning about self-advocacy

Finding out about and learning the skills involved in self-advocacy is important. Some groups use a set of books called *Learning About Self-Advocacy* (Values Into Action, 1988). In the Cardiff area, there is the opportunity for people with learning disabilities to learn about self-advocacy by joining one of the groups which meet in community education centres. Members take part in a programme called 'Skills for Advocacy' and work towards gaining Open College Credits as they progress through the different units. Although this might appear to 'formalise' self-advocacy as more of a structured learning process, there is flexibility and members belonging to these groups obviously enjoy them.

Rules

There was general agreement that rules were important and that having rules helped groups to be more ordered and disciplined. Before adopting rules, '... we found it wasn't very controlled... that's when we decided to have rules... it has been better with the rules'.

Some groups had a written list of rules, in other groups the rules were unwritten, but everybody knew them. The rules included:

- one person speaking at a time
- not using bad language
- not shouting or talking too loudly
- respecting each other's opinions when we don't agree
- being on time
- having commitment
- dressing smartly, especially when meeting and talking to other people

- turning up to meetings on time or sending apologies when unable to attend
- getting along together and treating each other with respect.

Members of People First Cardiff and the Vale have also recently worked on producing an updated Constitution, written in a style that people can more easily understand.

Rules were seen as important in helping people to work together and stick together. Getting along together included socialising together, having fun and celebrating group achievements. Members of People First Cardiff and the Vale are also welcoming to new members, guests and other groups who visit them.

Working together also included doing things in a way with which members felt comfortable. For example, one person voiced his disagreement with those who chose to adopt radical protest like some people in the disability movement:

> *The thing about it is that they've spoilt it by wrongly protesting, tying themselves to trains and everything like that. They've spoilt it then because they're protesting all wrong... creating a breach of the peace.*

Instead he felt a more diplomatic course of action was preferable: 'if necessary, you've got to see an MP' or take other actions that are legal, such as writing letters. Many people with learning disabilities are not used to radical action and do not feel comfortable with it.

Indeed, many fear the consequences not only from those in authority and from service workers, but also from parents. For example, in one self-advocacy group elsewhere in Britain, members of a group received temporary support from a volunteer who was more used to radical action. Without the group's consent, 'strong' protest posters and letters were circulated complaining about a local supported employment scheme for people with learning disabilities. As a consequence, one woman was stopped from attending the self-advocacy group by her mother who was involved with the scheme.

Good Practice Point:

It is important that members of a self-advocacy group should be able to decide as a group, how they want to work together and stick together. Acting together collectively, as a group, helps people to feel confident and strong. It is also an important part of members being in control over what happens and feeling comfortable.

Good organisation

It is really goodly organised, I would say, and we are growing, we are still expanding...

The way that a group was organised and run was also frequently mentioned as important. This included having a treasurer, a secretary, and a good chairperson: '...we always have a good chairperson... that's half the battle, to have a good chairperson, because you must have order in the meeting.' The chairperson needed to be diplomatic and able to make sure that everyone had a chance of saying something - someone who gave everyone 'a fair crack of the whip.' Officers are elected on to the committee of People First Cardiff and the Vale by a ballot, either by a show of hands or pieces of paper:

Every so often we have an election. If we want a Secretary or a Chairperson or a Treasurer we vote for them. The Chairperson changes every so often. We give the Chairperson three times to chair and then we have a different Chairperson, but the Secretary goes on for a bit longer and the Treasurer...

Being well organised also meant having someone to help with writing letters and other administrative tasks such as making telephone calls, organising taxis for people, sorting out the money and so on. One of the members was employed for three hours a week helping the facilitators with the organisation and administration. However, she often worked many more hours than that, especially at busy times, but could not get paid any extra or it would affect her benefits.

Good support

The job of helping with writing letters, taking down notes at meetings, telephoning, sorting out the money, organising taxis, supporting people at meetings, helping to explain documents and so on was seen as a role for the facilitator or adviser, the person who helped to support the self-advocacy group. It was the facilitator's role to 'see to it that everything's running smoothly ...' Members were, at the same time, also supported to become more independent and to do as much as they could themselves.

Good Practice Point:
Successful, active self-advocacy is usually underpinned by good, facilitative support from an independent facilitator who is not employed by health or social services. However, although independent, paid support may be a preferred choice, this is not always possible. It is more important that a facilitator is committed and loyal to the group and that it is someone whom the members like and trust. A facilitator should also have an understanding, or be willing to learn about, the issues involved - for example, potential conflicts of interest. They should also support members to do as much of the work that is involved as possible and ensure the group is in control and in charge of what happens.

The role of the facilitator or adviser is not to take over, or tell people what to do. In the Cardiff area, most of the facilitators supporting self-advocacy groups have undergone an accredited training course and many facilitators are independent of the statutory health and social services that members receive. Being a facilitator or adviser is not easy, as has been acknowledged by other people writing about self-advocacy (Dowson and Whittaker, 1993; Sutcliffe and Simons, 1993). Training is invaluable if it gives an awareness of the issues, problems and conflicts that might be involved, and learning how to provide support which allows members to be in charge without the adviser taking over. However, the People First survey of self-advocacy in Wales (Ramcharan et al., 1996) found that only a third of groups had people supporting them who had received training specific to self-advocacy.

Money

Good support also includes financial support. In Wales, the All Wales Strategy has been an important source of funding for many self-advocacy groups. It has provided money to pay for facilitators, transport to help people get to meetings, paid support for self-advocacy representatives attending service planning meetings, meeting room charges, postage, stationery, telephone calls and so on. Supporting self-advocacy involves costs that can soon mount up: *'We were on about the cost of taxis a little while ago... it's very expensive...'*

The People First survey suggested there was a strong relationship between funding and wider self-advocacy participation and representation in Wales, for example at service planning meetings at local and county levels. Many self-advocacy groups have received relatively generous funding under the All Wales Strategy which groups have come to rely on.

However, there are concerns that funding for self-advocacy may not continue in the future. Money that used to be set aside for people with learning disabilities is no longer 'ring-fenced' or protected just for them. Also, local government reorganisation (Wales was split from 8 counties to 22 unitary authorities in 1996) has left some authorities with less money.

Many self-advocacy groups find it difficult to gain access to funding. Not all self-advocacy groups have funds to help them grow and develop. This can affect their ability to work effectively as a group and can also affect their wider participation and representation.

Good Practice Point:
Self-advocacy groups need help and support in gaining access to funding. The new unitary authorities in Wales and elsewhere could assist by helping groups to access non-statutory funding and by recognising the importance of self-advocacy through statutory funding support.

Getting more people involved

Encouraging new members and getting more people interested in self-advocacy was also seen as an essential part of making self-advocacy work. This included thinking about how to attract more people, making self-advocacy more interesting and also how to include more people with physical, sensory and profound disabilities: 'we can use more braille cards... and talk more slowly... and deaf people can use the picture cards'. There was also recognition of the need for accessible venues that people could get to easily and that had wheelchair access 'as there are some people who can't walk.' Attracting more members was done by word of mouth, publicity and sometimes by advertising in the local press. As more people with learning disabilities joined self-advocacy groups, and more groups were started, there was also a need for more people to help facilitate and support groups, and more funding.

Getting more people involved also meant getting the positive support of people working in health, social services and education - as well as parents who needed reassurance that self-advocacy was beneficial for their adult sons and daughters.

Good Practice Point:
Spreading the word to attract new members means making sure information about self-advocacy is easy to understand and accessible for people who cannot read. New ways need to be explored to include more people with additional sensory, physical and more profound disabilities. Information about self-advocacy should be circulated to places where people with learning disabilities can find out about it. People should be helped to find out about self-advocacy and how they can get involved.

Problems and Difficulties

As shown in the preceding sections, self-advocacy is not all 'plain sailing'. Members of People First Cardiff and the Vale have had to work hard to confront and address problems and difficulties together. It is only by doing this that they have succeeded. 'Not being listened to', 'not being taken seriously' and continuing to be discriminated against because of the label 'learning disability' are common problems that are faced by many self-advocacy groups. In meeting with members of People First Cardiff and the Vale a number of problems were identified as shown in the figure (p.55).

Good Practice Point:
Confronting and overcoming the problems and difficulties faced by self-advocacy groups is a collective responsibility. Groups need to talk about the problems and difficulties they face so that they can work together to try and overcome them. They also need to make other people aware so that other people can try to help as well.

Looking Ahead to the Future

I think if we're working towards a new future, we're working for the next millennium to come. It's important to keep self-advocacy going.

Members of People First Cardiff and the Vale have worked hard in developing their membership, identity, organisational rules and support arrangements. This has allowed them to both 'speak up' and 'act', as a result of which they have already achieved many things. However, the work involved never ends. In looking ahead to the next millennium, members talked about some of their ideas for the future:

- Continuing the work of self-advocacy, speaking up for the rights of people with learning disabilities and continuing to campaign against and fight discrimination.

- Spreading the word about self-advocacy by having 'some sort of self-advocacy outreach' and going into schools and other places such as pubs and churches.

- Getting more funding, such as applying to the lottery.

- Buying a minibus to cut down on taxi costs.

- Getting 'our own base in which to work...' equipped with a typewriter and a computer and having training about how to use them.

Problems

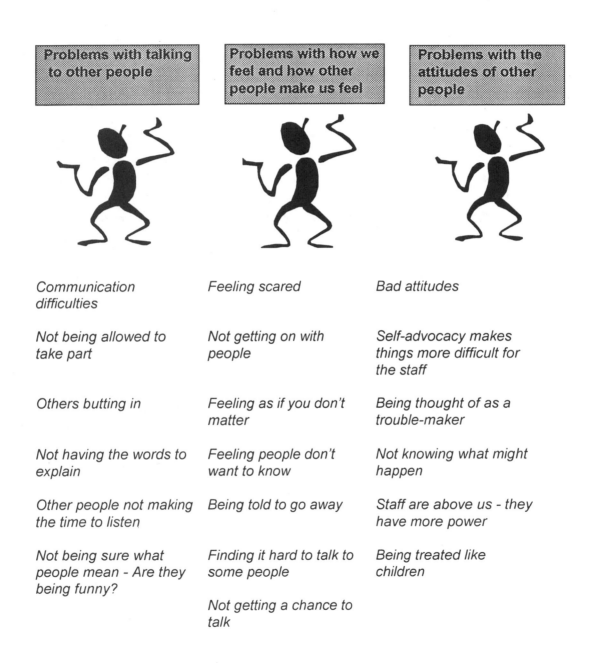

Problems with talking to other people	**Problems with how we feel and how other people make us feel**	**Problems with the attitudes of other people**
Communication difficulties	*Feeling scared*	*Bad attitudes*
Not being allowed to take part	*Not getting on with people*	*Self-advocacy makes things more difficult for the staff*
Others butting in	*Feeling as if you don't matter*	*Being thought of as a trouble-maker*
Not having the words to explain	*Feeling people don't want to know*	*Not knowing what might happen*
Other people not making the time to listen	*Being told to go away*	*Staff are above us - they have more power*
Not being sure what people mean - Are they being funny?	*Finding it hard to talk to some people*	*Being treated like children*
	Not getting a chance to talk	

- Helping to create employment for people as the self-advocacy movement grows stronger.

- Getting the voice of people with learning disabilities heard on more community groups and committees. For example, People First Cardiff and the Vale is a member of the Disabilities Issues Consultative Group, which is part of a Cardiff County Council Sub-Committee for Equal Opportunities. Amongst other things, the Group is campaigning for more workplaces and public transport to be made accessible.

- Meeting, talking and working with other like-minded groups, for example by inviting other groups to visit, or visiting them, and attending self-advocacy conferences.   For example, some members of the Bristol Self-advocacy Research Group recently visited. Both groups asked each other questions and shared information. The Bristol group also told members of People First Cardiff and the Vale about Europe People First, which is finding out about self-advocacy and people with learning disabilities in Europe.

Ultimately, though, self-advocacy is only a means to an end. In the future, members also hoped they would be able to move on from belonging to a self-advocacy group as it would no longer be necessary when they had achieved equal rights and paid jobs.   In the meantime, members are working towards becoming more independent and doing more things for themselves. Working together as people first they are 'working to make people understand what we all want out of life'.

Acknowledgements

The illustration on p. 41 is adapted from an original by John Carter, first published in Simons, K., (1993) *Sticking up for yourself: self-advocacy and people with learning difficulties*. University of Bristol: Norah Fry Research Centre.

References

Dowson, S. and Whittaker, A. (1993) *On One Side: The role of the adviser in supporting self-advocacy.* London: Values Into Action in association with the King's Fund Centre.

Ramcharan, P., Whittell, B., Thomas, B. and White, J. (1996) *The Growing Voice in Wales: People with a Learning Difficulty and Self-Advocacy in Wales.* Bangor: People First N.E. Wales in association with the Centre for Social Policy Research and Development, University of Wales, Bangor.

Sutcliffe, J. and Simons, K. (1993) *Self-Advocacy and Adults with Learning Difficulties.* Leicester: The National Institute of Adult Continuing Education.

Values Into Action (1988) *Learning About Self-advocacy.* London: Values Into Action.

Welsh Office (1983) *The All Wales Strategy for the Development of Services for Mentally Handicapped People.* Cardiff: Welsh Office.

Whittaker, A. (ed.) (1991) *Supporting Self-Advocacy.* London: The King's Fund Centre.

Bridget Whittell is a research officer at the Centre for Social Policy Research and Development at the University of Wales, Bangor. Much of her work and research interests are focused around advocacy and empowerment issues for people with learning disabilities. She has close involvement with a self-advocacy group based in the N.W. of England.

Paul Ramcharan is a senior lecturer at the University of Sheffield. Amongst his work interests has been a focus on empowerment and advocacy issues for people with learning disabilities.

Cardiff People First and the Vale is a self-advocacy forum with a membership representing different self-advocacy groups in the counties of Cardiff and the Vale of Glamorgan. As well as working to provide opportunities for as many people as possible to get involved in self-advocacy, the forum is active in promoting the rights of people with learning disabilities. The activities of members include training, conference organisation, newsletter production, lobbying, planning, resource management and representation on a number of groups and committees.

Contact addresses

Centre for Social Policy,
  Research & Development
University of Wales
Bangor
Gwynedd LL57 2DG
Wales

People First Cardiff and the Vale
c/o DART
The Friary Centre
The Friary
Cardiff CF1 4AA
Wales

4 From Social Clubs to Social Movement
Landmarks in the Development of the International Self-Advocacy Movement

Hank Bersani Jr.

Defining a Social Movement

> *The time may be ripe for the disabled to generate a social movement patterned after the at least partially successful examples of the Black Movement and the Women's Movement.* (Safilios-Rothchild, 1976, p 45)

Social science literature offers several approaches to defining a social movement. In a sense, a social movement may be like the quote about good art - hard to define, but one knows it on sight. Safilios-Rothchild (1976), above, refers to the well known 'women's Movement' and 'black movement' in the USA. Ironically, as her call for a disability movement was being penned, the movement was in fact being born.

Johnson, Larana and Gusfield (1994) offer criteria for a modern social movement. In a social movement, they suggest, members go beyond their typical social roles. A social movement represents a strong ideological change. Social movements involve the emergence of a new dimension of identity, often drawing upon a characteristic formerly seen as a weakness.

In the self-advocacy movement, as individuals who have grown up with the label of 'mental retardation' or 'mental handicap' form organisations, take on leadership roles, and demand policy changes, they are clearly going beyond the social role of 'mentally retarded'.

Shakespeare (1983) indicates that a major activity of the disabiiity rights movement has been the development of a positive identity and group consciousness. This can be seen in the specific successes of the self-advocacy movement. Organisations now insist on 'People First Language', and refuse to accept what they call the 'R' word ('retarded'). This is clear evidence of action - and success in escaping the role of the victim as described by William Ryan (1972). The idea that people with disabilities are 'people first' represents a radical ideological change. What was once a weakness (a cognitive impairment that required supervision and control by others) is now a strength (greater identity with others in oppressed lives that professionals will never understand).

People's Organisations

Alinski (1946) uses the phrase 'people's organizations' to describe social movements that use collective and individual action to create change. He describes two types of change: instrumental change that seeks change in direct services, and political/social change which seeks to change broad social assumptions. These organisations are composed of people who come together across previous political differences to generate power and develop new social orders. Social movements, especially 'people's organizations', have a tradition of direct action, doing activities to call attention to the cause and putting themselves on the line. Self-advocacy organisations on both sides of the Atlantic have learned the lessons of direct action.

In Britain, Shakespeare (1983) reports on direct actions by disability groups. The Campaign for Accessible Transport (CAT) and the Campaign Against Patronage (CAP) included visible actions such as protesters chaining their wheelchairs to buses and 'blockades' of telethon fund raisers that focus on pity. Hersov (1996) describes self-advocates' efforts in England to successfully challenge the childish logo of the parent association MENCAP - a sad-faced little boy known as 'Little Stephen'. The section on 'The Colorado Springs Uprising' below gives an account of direct action taken by People First of Colorado. These efforts seek both instrumental change - improved services and social change – and a shift in power.

Revolutionary Leadership and Organising for Empowerment

Freire (1986) describes the task of liberation as to no longer be prey to the system. Social leaders are called upon to reflect on the current world order and to transform it. The movement then does not try to improve the existing fabric by tailoring the social garment. Rather a liberation movement seeks to cut a whole new garment from new cloth. Mondros and Wilson (1994) describe types of goals for organisations interested in social change and empowerment as leadership development, enhanced organisational power, instrumental change and public education.

Viewed as a struggle for liberation, the self-advocacy movement bears strong resemblance to the struggles in the USA for women's rights, including the right to vote, and the civil rights of racial minorities, including again the right to vote. In many states today, self-advocacy organisations run voter registration drives to register voters with disabilities much as was done with women and people from black and minority ethnic groups in our not too distant past. Efforts to gain representation (voting seats) on boards of directors and the bodies that control services represent a struggle for suffrage as well.

The Last Civil Rights Movement?

Many professionals are at a loss to describe the phenomenon of self-advocacy by disabled individuals, especially by people who were said to have 'mental retardation'. We were comfortable when their organisations were social clubs. Some were bemused by their growing interests in organisational skills. Today, we cannot ignore their emerging power. Whether we look for ideological change, revolutionary leadership, or organising for power, the fact is that what we have come to call the 'self-advocacy movement' meets the definitions of a social movement.

From Social Clubs to Social Movement

Swedish origins

In the USA, the origins of the self-advocacy movement are usually attributed to a small group in Salem, Oregon who, in 1973 are credited with formulating the phrase: 'We are people first' (Perske, 1996; Edwards, 1982). However, unknown to them and their advisers, the roots of the movement go back several years earlier. Beginning in 1965 in Sweden, social clubs called 'flamslattsklubben' were being used to promote social training in Sweden for 'the adolescent retardate' (Nirje, 1969). Nirje described these social activities as 'hidden social training' of young adults. He saw them as a way to achieve what he called normalisation; one means of providing them with 'an existence, as close to the normal one as possible.' At this early stage, the educational value of social activity for 'the mentally retarded' was clear. His club activities would have been recognised by many special educators as an innovative approach to developing the social skills of many young people in special education services. Only two years later, Nirje reported training social club members in basic parliamentary procedure - a skill that only has use in the context of organising (Dybwad, 1996). As Beechey, Claesen and Nappi (1971) noted: 'integration in Swedish clubs means that the mentally retarded adolescents are active members, and as such, are encouraged to use their initiative and to assume increasing responsibilities for their own affairs'.

USA clubs

In Massachusetts, there are two parallel social clubs: one for men (the Mohawks) and one for women (the Squaws). Originally conceived in 1967 as a social club, members socialised, then learned social skills, then became interested in social issues (*Exceptional Parent*, 1978). The clubs continue today, and often offer their services (for a fee) as consultants on matters of disability services. Along the way, they learned how to run meetings like their Swedish counterparts.

Danish parallels

Similarly, in Denmark, early sports clubs for people with intellectual disabilities run by the National Association for Handicapped Sports, evolved into opportunities to study democracy and ultimately into self-advocacy activities referred to as 'Culture Conferences': organisations that conduct demonstrations and direct political action to influence public policy regarding services for people with intellectual disabilities.

The first such 'Culture Conference' was held in 1987 and included two delegates from each of 16 regions. Called a 'Culture Conference' to draw attention to the fact that people with disabilities felt left out of the cultural mainstream, they took on a role much like self-advocacy conferences in the USA. In the USA, many of these fledgling organisations have been associated with existing parent organisations such as The Arc. Similarly, in Denmark, the Culture Conference was supported by Landsforeningen Evnesvages Vel (the Danish parents' organisation). By the 1990s these meetings involved several hundred individuals learning about their rights, taking a position on disability policies and promoting local activities.

Characteristics of a Social Movement

In reviewing the history of the international self-advocacy movement, themes can be identified that support the idea that self-advocacy represents a new social movement with history, principles, organisation, conceptual reform, language, solidarity, justice and alliances.

History

A social movement writes its own history and identifies its roots. A social movement has identifiable early leaders and figureheads. As the first generation of the history of this movement is still being written, the names of charismatic individuals viewed as synonymous with the movement are yet to be determined by history. However, the allies of Rosemary and Gunnar Dybwad, Robert Perske, and Benjt Nirje are sure to be included. Lists of early leaders of the movement will surely include Barbara Goode, Åke Johanson, Debbie Allen, Bernard Carabello and others too numerous to recount here. Historians include Edwards (1982); Williams and Shoultz (1982) and Dybwad (1996).

Principles

A social movement has a manifesto and produces organising manuals and handbooks. As early as the 1970s, People First of Oregon was producing manuals on how to develop self-advocacy groups - mostly mimeographed, unpublished and distributed to anyone who was interested. Later, with the assistance of a federal grant at the University of Kansas, a project called United Together developed a series of handbooks and manuals - more professionally designed and sold through a publications list.

More recently, the International League of Societies for Persons with Mental Handicaps (1996) published *The Beliefs, Values and Principles of Self-Advocacy.* A committee of seven self-advocates from seven nations on three continents formulated a compelling manifesto of the movement.

Organisation

A social movement calls for equal representation for members, forms new organisations, and develops a national and international structure. From humble beginnings self-advocacy organisations are now functioning at the local, state and national levels in the USA, Canada, Australia, Britain, Norway, Sweden, Denmark, and more. In the USA, in 1992, representatives from the major state self-advocacy projects formed Self Advocates Becoming Empowered, the first national organisation for self-advocates (Shoultz and Ward, 1996). The rise of these various local and national organisations are well documented in Williams and Shoultz (1982), and in Dybwad and Bersani (1996).

Conceptual reform

A social movement demands to eliminate stereotypes and works to offer new definitions. Members name their own movement and promote change by offering a different perspective on social events. People who were 50 years ago described as 'feebleminded' are now seen as self-advocates (Dybwad, 1996). Self-advocates, whose social roles had previously been as 'the retarded' or 'clients' are now seen as advocates, teachers and trainers. People who, a few years ago, were seen as being dependent upon others and recipients of support, are now seen as advocacy allies and even leaders. The self-advocacy movement represents a sweeping ideological change. Once considered to be MR (mentally retarded), Barb Goode says that in fact the initials MR really indicate that she is 'Mighty Remarkable' (Goode, 1996). Self-advocates are taking over agendas and redefining issues. Speaking at an international congress, one self-advocate stated: 'Next Congress we would like to meet again to explain what it means to be mentally handicapped and what it does not mean.'

Language

A social movement makes good use of rhetoric. A movement develops its own literature and lore. It has its own anthems, poets and troubadours. It uses slogans and songs effectively to crystallise its agenda. Some movements use simple elegance - a bumper sticker reading 'Free Tibet' tells the reader volumes about the views of the vehicle owner. Buttons and T-shirts that proclaim the slogans of the self-advocacy movement include 'We speak for ourselves!' 'Nothing about me without me'.

Actions to reform the language of others include the concept of 'People First language' and efforts to eliminate the use of the term 'mental retardation', often referred to as the 'R' word. In the USA self-advocates can be credited with name changes to the national parent organisation, from National Association for Retarded *Children*, to Association for Retarded *Citizens*, and then again to *The Arc* (with lower-case letters to indicate that the name is no longer an acronym). Likewise, the popularity of People First language has lead to changes in the authors' guidelines to several professional journals including the *American Journal on Mental Retardation*, *Mental Retardation* and *The Journal of the Association for People with Severe Handicaps*.

In the USA, Robert Williams has functioned as the first poet laureate of the self-advocacy movement. Although his disabilities are not cognitive, his written voice clearly articulates the experiences of many. Karl Williams, folk singer, has become the wandering minstrel of the movement, composing songs of the struggle and singing them at meetings across the USA to rally members of the movement and to remind all who will listen of the issues at hand. In Canada, Dennis LaRouch composes and performs songs of his struggle and those of the movement. His composition *Le National* is the anthem for the Canadian movement.

Solidarity

A social movement supports self-identification and raises consciousness among members and in society. Members advocate on behalf of others, not just themselves. They identify and validate common formative experiences. They raise the consciousness of members and outsiders alike.

Self-advocates share common stories of having their concerns dismissed, their talents ignored. Åke Johanson (1996) writes of 'Handicapped consciousness' and the importance of first understanding one's own handicap before moving into social action. Self-advocacy conferences provide, among more social functions, a chance for people to share their common experiences of institutionalisation, abuse and neglect. Many self-advocacy meetings provide opportunities for old friends to be reunited after years of separations due to the vagaries of institutional transfers and often hurried deinstitutionalisation that disrupted friendships and families. While visiting with a self-advocacy group in Australia, I met two members who told me that although they were brother and sister, they grew up in separate institutions, unaware of each other. Decades later, they met at a self-advocacy sponsored dance and realised their family ties.

Justice

Social movements seek justice and representation. DeJong (1983) points out that disability groups have resorted to direct action, including civil disobedience only after exhausting traditional legal avenues. Self-advocacy groups led the search for justice in Canada in the sterilisation case of a woman with learning difficulties known as 'Eve' (Goode, 1996).

The self-advocates took to action after parent and professional organisations found the topic too controversial to address. Historically men and women labelled 'mentally handcapped' had often been sterilised without their permission. As a result of the 'Eve' case and thanks to the efforts of People First leaders in Canada, the Supreme Court there decided 'no-one will be sterilized without their permission' (Kappel, 1996). In the USA in 1991, when People First of Tennessee sued the state to close an institution, once again the self-advocates led the way in the notable absence of professional and parent organisation action (Beckwith, 1996). In Nashville, People First of Tenessee went before the US District court to bring a law suit against the Governor of the State, the Superintendent of one of the state mental retardation institutions, the Tennessee Department of Mental Health and Retardation, the Tennessee Department of Health, and the Tennessee Department of Human Services. They were not joined initially by The Arc (the parents association) or AAMR (the professional association), or any of the University or well known legal advocacy organisations in the state. The suit alleged that the conditions in the institution were illegal and asked for the institution to be closed, not simply improved.

Alliances

Social movements build alliances with sympathetic organisations but also wrestle with the role of formative segregation. Black people may seek integration, but hold black-only events to build identity. The women's movement seeks equality but still holds women-only events. Many social movements seeking social integration continue to find use for what might be seen as segregated events.

Likewise, self-advocates participate in members-only events. Many self-advocacy meetings are closed to non-members. The 1998 International People First Conference in Alaska was run by self-advocates and only allowed non-disabled presenters as co-presenters on panels led by self-advocates.

G. Allan Roeher, founder of the Canadian National Institute on Mental Retardation that now bears his name, understood early on the need for self-advocates to control their own destinies. In 1978 he acknowledged the specialised roles of various groups: parents, professionals, citizen advocates and self-advocates. 'Only mentally retarded (sic) people can organise themselves in People First organisations' (Dybwad, 1996). His words contain several messages in almost haiku form. He indicates the need for not just disability organisations, but intellectual disability groups. He also indicates the need for parents, friends, allies and even advisers to stand back and allow the key players - the individuals with intellectual disabilities to do the organising.

Principles into Action

There are numerous examples that demonstrate the power of the movement. I have selected just two 'action profiles' to demonstrate how these various principles combine in the social action of the self-advocacy movement.

The Colorado Springs Uprising: self-advocates seek system solution

In 1988 in Colorado Springs, Colorado, a group of self-advocates made it clear that their organisation was not just a social club. Their services (and their lives) were controlled by a state-wide network of 'Community Center Boards' (CCBs) that provided services. However, only two of the twenty CCBs had representation by direct consumers on their boards of directors.

On August 4th, 1988 the group chose direct action. They marched on a board meeting with placards and slogans. The headline in the paper the next day read: 'Disabled protest board makeup: Group wants representation on funding panel' (Cotton, 1988). Debbie Allen, President of People First of Colorado, interviewed at the protest, said: 'We want three direct consumers on this board'. Carrying signs that said: 'We won't be shut up or shut out', Ms. Allen pointed out that the group had been working for ten months to get representation on the board. When their efforts consistently failed, they made the decision to engage in civil disobedience and take over the public meeting. When the board meeting closed down to close them out, Allen and her associates took over the chairs of the board officers and held an impromptu press conference.

Although the Court ultimately decided against the group, they have created dramatic social change. The protests were covered in several local papers. A decade later, the number of boards with some level of direct consumer participation is hugely increased. Meanwhile, several states away, the Illinois State Legislature has passed legislation mandating consumer participation known as the Persons with Disabilities on State Agency Boards Act (Ficker-Terrill, 1992). Direct action leads to social change.

Five days that said it all: The Third International People First Conference

Where else can you see a young man from Stillwater, Oklahoma sitting alongside someone from Tokyo while nearby there are French and English-speaking Canadians discussing human rights issues with a woman from Germany, while an American Sign Language interpreter is translating furiously? How much more unlikely is the scenario if all the people involved have grown up with the label 'mental retardation'?

For five days, June 25th - 29th, 1993, at a conference in Toronto, 1400 people, most of whom bore the label 'mental retardation' came together from 32 different nations around the world to discuss the issues around 'intellectual disability'. The universality of the issues and concerns raised by the participants was striking. Men from Japan, women from Australia, people with mild intellectual impairments from England and people with severe and multiple disabilities from the USA all raised the same set of issues, each in their own language and each with their own communication style. The quest for dignity, privacy, contact with friends, sexuality, being seen as adult and a search for a home of one's own was pervasive.

For many of the participants this was their first time so far from home. However, for others, international travel was old hat in spite of their disabilities. A Canadian self-advocate for example, was looking for friends that she had met on previous trips to Rio de Janeiro, Nairobi and Paris.

The theme of the conference was 'a celebration of successes' and there were countless such stories recounted. They included moving out of institutions, getting out of special classes, meeting and marrying the love of one's life and getting a home of one's own.

One man told his own story about growing up disabled. Although he was in a special class in school, he never learned to read and he graduated without a regular diploma. As a young adult he still could not read and had difficulty getting jobs. Then he married and had a child. He spoke of realising how important it was that someone read to his child each night. However, this task fell only to his wife because she was able to read and he was not. He wanted to learn to read so he got involved with an adult literacy program and did so. He can read to his child now and has a job at the Holiday Inn that he could not get previously because the job required literacy skills that were beyond him. This is a testament to the power of motivation.

However, the sweetness of success is measured against some sorrow. At the start of the second day, the plenary session was filled with 1400 people of varying ages, nationalities, languages and intellectual abilities. As the presentations proceeded, there was the expected level of 'background noise' of side conversations and impromptu translations into the various languages of the day. Suddenly, speaking in a loud clear voice from the podium, a self-advocate addressed the crowd. He called for a moment of silence, in memory of all of those who had died in institutions. The crowd rose to their feet, joined hands, bowed heads and stood in absolute silence, for two minutes. The silence was a stark counterpoint to the noise level a few minutes ago and the attention to those who had died contrasted starkly with the wonderful success stories of those fortunate enough to be at the meeting.

A recurring theme in the conference was that of 'labelling'. Individuals from various countries wrestled with the issue of what to call people, including each other. None of the participants indicated any support for the term 'mental retardation'. Some preferred 'mental handicap', others preferred 'intellectual disability'; still others insisted on the phrase 'learning difficulties'. A particularly moving moment in the conference was when Barb Goode received the first Rosemary Dybwad Award for Women Self-Advocates. Her work in organising the Canadian group, as well as her international efforts, were praised. The long list of Ms. Goode's accomplishments included the fact that in 1992 she was the first self-advocate to address the General Assembly of the United Nations. The award, in memory of the late Dr. Rosemary Dybwad, also commemorated Rosemary Dybwad's life-long dedication to people with disabilities and her international activities. Ms. Goode thanked her self-advocate friends and then turned the 'labelling' tables by also thanking the many 'normates' who had helped her over the years.

Noticeably lacking from the topics discussed were those often on the agenda at conferences *about* mental retardation. There was no mention of how to modify undesired behavior, or how to control 'aggressive clients'. There were no sessions on the relative merits of electric shock versus 'differential reinforcement of incompatible behaviors'. Not even any sessions about the economics of reducing institutional populations. This conference was about joyous celebration and dignified memorials, recognition of how far the movement had come and recognition that the accomplishments to date were only the beginning. No longer just a type of instructional social club, self-advocacy was clearly an international social movement.

References

Alinski, S.D. (1946) *Reveille for radicals.* New York,: Random House.

Beckwith (1996) The Bruises are on the Inside: An Advisers' Perspective. In Dybwad, G. and Bersani, H. (eds.) (see below).

Beechey, M., Claeson, I, and Nappi, M.L. (1971) *'The youth volunteer': Report of International Symposium on volunteers.* Washington DC, USA: Department of Health, Education & Welfare.

Bramley, J and Elkins, J. (1988) Some issues in the development of self-advocacy among persons with intellectual disabilities. *Australia and New Zealand Journal of Developmental Disabilities, 14,* 147 - 157.

Cotton (1988) Disabled protest board make-up. Colorado, *Gazette Telegraph*, August 5, B1-2.

DeJong, G. (1983) Defining and implementing the independent living concept. In Crewe, N.M., Zola, I.K., et al. *Independent living for physically disabled people.* San Francisco: Jossey-Bass.

Driedger, D. (1989) *The last civil rights movement: Disabled People's International.* London: Hurst & Co.

Dybwad, G. and Bersani, H. (eds.) (1996) *New voices: self-advocacy by people with disabilities*. Cambridge, Massachusetts: Brookline Books.

Dybwad, G. (1996) Setting the stage historically. In Dybwad, G. and Bersani, H. (eds.).

Edwards, J. (1982) *We are people first: our handicaps are secondary*. Oregon: Ednick Inc.

Exceptional Parent (1978) Mohawks and Squaws. A social club. Psy-Ed-Corp. 13-17.

Ficker-Terrill, K. (1992) Illinois passes legislation mandating consumer participation. *AAMR news and notes*, 6, (5).

Freire, P. (1986) *Pedagogy of the oppressed* (Reprint). Harmondsworth: Penguin.

Goode, B. (1996) It's been a struggle: Her own story. In Dybwad, G. and Bersani, H. (eds.).

Hersov, J. (1996) The rise of self-advocacy in Britain. In Dybwad, G. and Bersani, H. (eds.).

International League of Societies for Persons with Mental Handicaps (ILSMH) (1996) *The beliefs, values and principles of self-advocacy*. Cambridge, Massachusetts: Brookline Books.

Johnson, Å. (1996) Handicap consciousness. In Dybwad, G. and Bersani, H. (eds.).

Johnson, H., Larana, E. and Gusfield, J.R. (1994) *New social movements from ideology to identity*. Philadelphia: Temple University Press.

Kappel, B. (1996) A history of People First in Canada. In Dybwad, G. and Bersani, H. (eds.).

Mondros, J.B. and Wilson, S.W. (1994) *Organizing for power and empowerment.* New York: Columbia University Press.

Nirje, B. (1969) The normalisation principle and its human management implications. In Kugel, R. and Wolfensberger, W. (eds.) *Changing Patterns in residential services for the mentally retarded.* Washington: President's Committee on Mental Retardation.

Nirje, B. (1972) The right to self-determination. In Wolfensberger, W. (ed.) *The principle of normalization.* Toronto, Canada: National Institute of Mental Retardation.

Perske, R. (1972) The dignity of risk and the mentally retarded. *Mental Retardation, 10,* 1-12.

Perske, R. (1996) Self-advocates on the move: A journalist's view. In Dybwad, G. and Bersani, H. (eds.).

Rhoades, C.M. (1986) Self-Advocacy. In Wortis, J. (ed.), *Mental retardation and developmental disabilities,* (vol. XIV). New York, USA: Elsevier Science Publishing Co.

Rivera, G. (1972) *Willowbrook: A report on how it is and why it does not have to be that way.* New Hampshire, USA: Vantage Books.

Ryan, W. (1972) *Blaming the victim.* New York: Vintage Books.

Safilios-Rothchild (1976) Disabled persons' self-definitions and their implications for rehabilitation. In Abrecht, G.L. (ed.) The sociology of physical disability and rehabilitation. Pittsburgh, Philadelphia: University of Pittsburgh Press.

Shakespeare, T. (1993) Disabled people's self-organisation: a new social movement? *Disability, Handicap and Society, 8,* 3.

Shoultz, B. and Ward, N. (1996) Self-advocates becoming empowered. In Dybwad, G. and Bersani, H. (eds.).

Williams, P and Shoultz, B. (1982). *We can speak for ourselves.* London: Souvenir Press.

Hank Bersani, Jr. is currently on the faculty of the Oregon Health Sciences University where he holds appointments in the Department of Public Heath and Preventive Medicine and in the Department of Pediatrics. A long time ally of self-advocates, he is a regular speaker at self-advocacy events and routinely involves self-advocates in the training he conducts. His recent publications include Dybwad, G. and Bersani, H, (eds.) (1996) *New Voices: Self-advocacy by people with disabilities.* Cambridge MA, USA: Brookline Books. He is currently editing a volume written entirely by people who use augmentative communication, to be published by Paul Brookes Publishers.

Contact address
Oregon Institute on Disability and Development
Oregon Health Sciences University
P.O. Box 574
Portland
Oregon 97207-0574, U.S.A.

Section 3

Information for Empowerment

5 Information is Power
The Impact of Accessible Information on People with Learning Difficulties

Ruth Townsley

We live in a society that relies upon the printed word. Through printed information we communicate with others and are informed about issues that affect us. For the majority of people with learning difficulties, however, a society that relies on printed information is a society that excludes them. Estimates suggest that a very high proportion of people with learning difficulties do not have literacy skills. For example, a verbal poll of 70 people attending a Bristol Adult Training Centre discovered that 60 could not read or write. The Adult Literacy and Basic Skills Unit also points out that 6.5 million adults in England and Wales have literacy difficulties (Gregory, 1996). Therefore for people with learning difficulties, having access to information in an understandable form is something that is integral to any notion of empowerment or self-advocacy.

Access to information in appropriate formats is a human rights issue. People with learning difficulties have a right to receive information in a form they can understand (Roeher, 1991). As People First, a user-led organisation for people with learning difficulties, puts it:

> *Big words keep us out.*
> (People First Newsletter, No.3, 1993, p.6)

In the UK, there is now a growing awareness of the importance of providing easy to understand public information in a variety of formats. Organisations like the Plain English Campaign have argued for the public's right to clearer information for many years. Indeed, the Disability

Discrimination Act 1995 prohibits providers of all goods and services to discriminate against disabled people; these 'service providers' include providers of information and community services. User-led groups of people with learning difficulties, like People First and Change, are also advocating for material that is easier to understand (e.g. People First, 1997; Change, 1997).

The field of disability research is currently making efforts to move towards a more emancipatory approach, where the involvement of disabled researchers and consultants is accepted as central to the success of any research project. In the field of learning difficulties, the participation of people with learning difficulties in research can only be fully achieved if information about research is made accessible to everyone. In addition, if the findings of research are to have any direct impact on the lives of those they concern, there is a moral obligation for researchers to make their publications easier to understand.

The Plain Facts Project

The Joseph Rowntree Foundation is a key funder of UK-based social research concerning learning difficulties. The Foundation currently publishes a clear, concise *Findings* paper from each project that it supports (see, for example, Townsley and Macadam, 1996). Foundation staff were aware, however, that the existing format of *Findings* was not accessible to people with learning difficulties. In an attempt to meet this challenge, they commissioned the Norah Fry Research Centre to investigate ways of producing research findings in a format that people with learning difficulties would find easier to understand.

After eight months of pilot work and consultation, the *Plain Facts* magazine and audio tape were launched. The first series of eight issues ran from 1996 to 1997, followed by an evaluation based on comments from readers and listeners. *Plain Facts* is now published six times a year, with each issue focusing on the findings of a different research project. The defining feature of the research reported in *Plain Facts* is that the findings of each chosen project should be of interest to people with learning difficulties. To date, we have covered a wide range of subjects, including housing and support, choosing staff, leaving hospital, supported employment and making complaints. *Plain Facts* goes free to 1100 self advocacy groups and day centre groups across the UK. It is also available to other groups and individuals on a subscription basis.

The production of *Plain Facts* is very much a team effort. We employ an illustrator, a graphic designer and an audio tape producer who work together with me (the editor) to put *Plain Facts* on paper and on to audio tape. Using a combination of clear language, illustrations and audio material, we then work with individual researchers (whose projects are the focus for *Plain Facts*) to make their research findings easier to understand. We expect researchers to have consulted with people with learning difficulties in order to develop their *Plain Facts* text. Guidance on this and on other issues is included in the fact sheet *Writing Plain Facts* that researchers receive as part of the Rowntree Foundation's standard documentation to new projects. We also ask researchers to provide suggestions for up to six illustrations. The illustrator, Jennifer Lauruol, is careful to incorporate a range of human characters within her pictures, including people from different black and minority ethnic groups, people using wheelchairs, people with multiple impairments, young people, older people, and so on.

Each *Plain Facts* magazine is four pages in length and will sometimes include one or two additional Fact Sheets. The front page gives space for up to six key points and one large illustration. The two inside pages expand on these points using sub-headings and up to four smaller illustrations. The back page usually has three sections. The first section on 'Things to do' suggests ideas for action and discussion based on the topic of the research. The second section on 'More information' gives details of other relevant materials for both people with learning difficulties and supporters - leaflets, videos, help-line numbers, useful organisations, learning materials. The final section - 'About the project' - includes names and photographs of the researchers involved in the project and the name, address and telephone number of a person who can provide more information about the research. The purpose of the extra Fact Sheets is to supplement specific sections of the main text, where additional detail is needed. This might include, for example, elaborating on an important point, defining a difficult word or phrase, or giving extra suggestions for learning activities or role-play ideas.

Until recently, the project has been guided by a small advisory group which included people with learning difficulties. From 1998, two groups will guide the work of the *Plain Facts* project: a management group will advise the *Plain Facts* team on editorial and organisational issues, and an editorial board will look at the text and illustrations and suggest changes or developments.

Evaluating Plain Facts

Publishing *Plain Facts* has been an exciting and challenging learning experience for all of the production team. It was particularly helpful for us to hear about what people with learning difficulties thought of *Plain Facts*. As part of a readership survey undertaken in 1996, we distributed a short questionnaire to 500 groups who had already received *Plain Facts*. The questionnaire consisted of 16 short questions each accompanied by an appropriate illustration. It was also recorded on to audio tape, with the reverse side left blank for a reply. Just over 50 questionnaires were returned to us by 1st October 1996. Of these, 33 were from client committees at local authority day services. Nine self-advocacy groups responded and we received a further nine replies from un-named groups. The questionnaire survey was followed up by face-to-face interviews with four of the respondent groups. We asked an independent researcher, who was not linked to the *Plain Facts* project, to undertake these interviews on our behalf.

Questions covered the distribution of *Plain Facts*, the support available to groups, the accessibility of *Plain Facts*, its design and layout, people's preferences in relation to the content and the impact of *Plain Facts* on its readers.

We also continue to gather information about the effectiveness of *Plain Facts* by logging all general comments and enquiries, and by asking the researchers involved to give their views on the experience of writing *Plain Facts*.

The impact of *Plain Facts*

We were genuinely surprised to discover that many people were using *Plain Facts* as a source of new information and for ideas about how to bring about action or change within their own lives.

Plain Facts as a source of new information

For over half of those who responded to the survey, *Plain Facts* told them something they did not already know. The area of new information mentioned most was employment, followed by adult education, benefits and making complaints. Several groups also mentioned that they had not previously known that they could have access to job trainers, service brokers or to independent advocates.

The importance of employment to people with learning difficulties was reflected in comments like these:

> *The one on employment was helpful. We want to get jobs.*

We didn't know that people with learning difficulties are able to get paid employment.

One person in our group had not understood that she could have asked for paid work.

We didn't know that you could have a helper at work or that you could lose benefits if you started work.

Several groups explained that they had found the section on 'More information' particularly helpful:

It was good to know about different subjects, videos and books.

It gives us the addresses of different organisations so that we can get more information if we want.

Some of the more general perceptions seemed to indicate that *Plain Facts* had shown some groups what was possible for people with learning difficulties:

We learnt a lot, it was very remarkable, it was interesting, it was good.

Gave us ideas about learning new things. Made us feel more positive.

It was useful for us to talk about things that we didn't realise were available to us.

Finally, several respondents who had not found out any new information said that *Plain Facts* had nevertheless been useful as a means of recapping on things they already knew:

It explained things for us again.

We didn't learn anything new but listening to the tape helped us to understand things better.

Plain Facts as a source of ideas for action and change

It is extremely difficult to quantify how far any publication in itself brings about change, or encourages people to do things that they had not previously considered. However, reading *Plain Facts* certainly seemed to have prompted some people into action.

We asked respondents if *Plain Facts* had given them any ideas about things to do; 28 groups said it had. We also received additional information about this area from general telephone and postal enquiries. The main area that had excited people's interest was housing - something covered by both *Plain Facts 1* and *2:*

> *One of the group members has made enquiries about moving out of his parents' home into a home of his own.*

> *It helped me think about setting up home with my girlfriend.*

> *I enjoyed Plain Facts. I read it at the Centre and then took it home to show my parents. We are going to set up a meeting with someone from social services to talk about finding me somewhere else to live.*

Making complaints was also something respondents seemed likely to do more of, as a direct result of *Plain Facts*:

> *We photocopied the Plain Facts on Complaints for everyone in the centre so they can make a complaint if they want.*

The *Plain Facts* on adult education and supported employment also seemed to have prompted action in some areas:

> *We are using the supported employment one to help us get jobs.*

> *The tape about work just really made me want to do it!*

> *Some of us would like to do different courses at college. We will talk to our community support worker about these things.*

Many people seemed to find *Plain Facts* useful as a starting point for finding out more about a particular subject:

We are going to ring for more information about jobs.

We've got lots of people to contact now. We are going to follow up the ideas in the videos and books and to invite people to come and talk to the group.

One group explained that *Plain Facts* had introduced them to the idea of research itself:

We didn't know what research was ... We are going to do our own piece of research now in the New Year asking employers in our area some questions like: 'Would you pay a worker with learning disabilities?' 'Would you have a worker with learning disabilities in your workplace?'

Some groups were also using *Plain Facts* as a discussion tool; one day centre had even set up a *Plain Facts* discussion group:

It helps us to talk together in a group, share our ideas and opinions.

The comments made by the groups who were interviewed echoed those made by survey respondents:

I didn't know I could have a flat of my own.

It made me start thinking about a lot of things.

It teaches us new things, especially about work itself and employment.

At the time we read it, it was very appropriate to the group because a number of people were actually thinking about looking for a job.

One group said that they would like to see examples of many more ideas and activities that they could do themselves:

We were excited after we read it. We wanted to take some of things further. But it was frustrating because we had to ask staff for help.

Future Developments

The evaluation of *Plain Facts* helped to highlight several areas that need further consideration. These included the distribution of *Plain Facts*, the nature of the support available to groups receiving *Plain Facts*, and the overall accessibility of the magazine and audio tape.

Distribution of *Plain Facts*

All of the groups we interviewed said that their copy of *Plain Facts* came in the post. Only two of the groups, however, actually opened the envelope themselves. Most groups kept the copies of *Plain Facts* in a special drawer, or folder, for future reference. Although all the groups knew where the copies of *Plain Facts* were kept, one group mentioned that they had to ask the day service manager for the key to the filing cabinet before they could actually get hold of a copy of *Plain Facts*. Putting *Plain Facts* under lock and key is hardly in keeping with the spirit of providing 'accessible' information. The future challenge for the production team is to try to find a way of encouraging supporters to store *Plain Facts* somewhere that is easily accessible to people with learning difficulties - i.e. not in a locked office!

Support to groups

Most respondents said that they read *Plain Facts* in a group with other people. Very few people read *Plain Facts* on their own. We had hoped that most groups of people with learning difficulties would have access to a supporter or facilitator. This was borne out by the survey findings - 36 groups said that someone helped them to read *Plain Facts*. For us this was a very useful finding, since *Plain Facts* is aimed at 'people with learning difficulties and their supporters'. We have chosen, for example, to include details of publications relevant to supporters as well as to people with learning difficulties themselves. It was also good to know that most groups have access to someone who can support them to take action or to find out more about a particular topic.

All of the groups we interviewed had a supporter who helped them to read *Plain Facts* and to listen to the tape. However, one supporter said that she did not regularly show the paper copy of *Plain Facts* to the group because 'no-one has literacy skills'. This is a disappointing finding, since this particular supporter had obviously not understood the relevance of using the pictures alongside the audio tape.

The next step for the production team is to find a way of encouraging supporters to make full use of the illustrations within *Plain Facts*, particularly with people who do not have literacy skills. Supporters may also wish to use the information and ideas set out in *Plain Facts* with people who have multiple impairments. This may mean using a range of additional and specific communication techniques in order to convey the material in the most appropriate way for that particular person.

Is *Plain Facts* easy to understand?

Overall, the people with learning difficulties we interviewed said that they found *Plain Facts* easy to understand:

> *It's simple to understand. There's no complicated dialect.*

However, as five groups pointed out, some issues of *Plain Facts* were easier to understand than others. One respondent also felt that listening to the tape helped make *Plain Facts* easier to understand. However, two people pointed out that *Plain Facts* is not accessible to everyone with learning difficulties, particularly people with multiple impairments:

I can understand what it's saying but some people can't.

We may have to accept that there are groups of people whom we cannot reach through *Plain Facts*. We hope, however, that by making *Plain Facts* available to all people with learning difficulties, the magazine may, in itself, act as a prompt to supporters so that they begin to discuss some of the issues covered by *Plain Facts* with people who need higher levels of support.

The audio tape

We asked people what they thought of the audio tape:

Very good. Very interesting. Very clear.

The music was good as well.

It would be good to have more voices on the tape and for people with learning difficulties to do some of the talking themselves.

Listening to the tape made it easier.

The fourth of these quotations highlights an issue that we hoped would be borne out by the findings of this study. Certainly it did seem that on its own, the tape provided an easy to understand form of information for most people who do not read. In conjunction with the paper copy of *Plain Facts*, the audio tape also helped to reinforce people's initial understanding of the magazine. Moreover, providing an audio taped version of a document helps to maintain people's interest in a topic - an important step towards enabling readers to use and act upon the information that they read.

There was one group, however, who had quite strong reservations about the effectiveness of the audio tape. They felt that the introductory music was too long and the musical page-turn markers were confusing. The members of this group did not read and therefore found it difficult to link the page-turn markers with the text. They suggested that some sort of written symbol on the magazine itself might be helpful in this respect.

The second series of *Plain Facts* has taken these comments on board. We have included the words 'now turn the page' on the audio tape, and plans are afoot to involve people with learning difficulties as speakers on the tape.

Which issue of *Plain Facts* did people prefer?

It was interesting to find out that *Plain Facts 6*, on 'College and Adult Education', was the most popular issue (17 mentions). This was followed by *Plain Facts 5*, on 'Supported Employment', and *Plain Facts 3*, on 'Making Complaints'. There may have been an element of bias, in that *Plain Facts 5* and *6* were sent out at the same time as the questionnaire, and would therefore have been the two most recently read issues.

Nevertheless there is a common feature amongst *Plain Facts 3, 5* and *6* in that they are based on projects which had very clear outcomes for people with learning difficulties themselves. They all also used plenty of quotes and real life examples to illustrate the main points. The use of quotations and case study material is fundamental to communicating a message to people with learning difficulties, especially in terms of its relevance to their lives. Clearly we should increase our efforts to find ways of incorporating more of this type of information into *Plain Facts*.

The Impact of Accessible Information

The findings from the *Plain Facts* postal survey and group interviews have demonstrated that there is a clear need for information that is easier to understand. The high number of respondents who said that *Plain Facts* had told them about something new, or had given them ideas about things to do, is indicative of the impact that accessible information can have on people's lives.

The fact that *Plain Facts* was the catalyst for discussion and action by groups and individuals is, in itself, extremely encouraging. However, *Plain Facts* also provided a means of enabling people with learning difficulties and their supporters to access research findings that were previously denied to them. Access to information should be a basic right but it is one that has only very recently been made available to people with learning difficulties. Yet, the move by many agencies towards increased user involvement in service planning and development can only truly be achieved where information about relevant issues is made available in formats that are accessible to everyone. Reports from people with learning difficulties that *Plain Facts* is helping them to talk about the implications of research in their day services and self-advocacy groups provides evidence of both an effective form of dissemination and of people's successful involvement in issues that affect their lives.

More information

Plain Facts (magazine and audio tape for adults with learning difficulties) is published by the Norah Fry Research Centre (see below). There are six issues of *Plain Facts* a year and it is free to user-led groups. Subscriptions are available for other individuals or organisations.

Writing Plain Facts is a fact sheet for supporters and researchers about how to write a *Plain Facts* magazine. You can get a free copy from the Norah Fry Research Centre (address below). Please send a stamped A4 sized self addressed envelope with your order.

Plain Facts: Information about research for people with learning difficulties is a short report about the *Plain Facts* project. It includes copies of the first eight issues of *Plain Facts* as well as a copy of the *Writing Plain Facts* fact sheet. You can get a copy from the Norah Fry Research Centre (Price £9.50).

Acknowledgements

Thanks to Jenni Lauruol for permission to reproduce her illustrations, which originally appeared in *About Plain Facts*, a fact sheet about the *Plain Facts* series, which is available free to people with learning difficulties from the Norah Fry Research Centre (address below).

References

Change (1997) *More Access Please.* London: Change.

Gregory, W. (1996) *The Informability Manual.* London: The Stationery Office.

People First (1997) *Access First. A Guide on How to Give Written Information for People with Learning Difficulties.* London: People First.

Roeher Institute (1991) *The Right to Read and Write: A Straightforward Guide to Literacy and People with Mental Handicap in Canada.* Ontario, Canada: Roeher Institute.

Townsley, R., and Macadam, M. (1996) 'Involving people with learning difficulties in staff recruitment'. *Social Care Research Findings* 91. York: Joseph Rowntree Foundation.

Ruth Townsley is a Research Fellow at the Norah Fry Research Centre, University of Bristol. She edits *Plain Facts*, a magazine about research for adults with learning difficulties. Ruth's current research work is focusing on support to children with complex health needs. Her other interests include user involvement in services and research and ways of making information more accessible to people with learning difficulties.

Contact address
Norah Fry Research Centre
University of Bristol
3 Priory Road
Bristol BS8 1TX
England

6 Working Together for Change
Involving People with Intellectual Disabilities in the Work of a Public Policy Research Institute

Miriam Ticoll

The Roeher Institute is Canada's national institute for the study of public policy affecting people with disabilities. The Institute was established over thirty years ago (then called the National Institute on Mental Retardation) as an arm of the advocacy organisation at that time known as The Canadian Association for the Mentally Retarded (now the Canadian Association for Community Living - CACL).

Over the past 30 years there have been considerable changes in the direction and philosophy of both organisations. CACL has evolved into an important lobbying and advocacy organisation with a national and international profile representing families and individuals with an intellectual disability.

In the last decade the focus of the research, information, education and social development activities of The Roeher Institute have broadened to encompass cross-disability issues within a human rights perspective that critically examines social policy trends provincially, nationally and globally. Although The Roeher Institute and CACL are now separate organisations, the ongoing close relationship of the two organisations has meant that there continues to be a strong emphasis at the Institute on understanding social change through the lens of what it means to live with a level of intellectual disability.

As a research institute, we at The Roeher Institute have been grappling for quite some time with the question of how to involve people with an intellectual disability in what we do in a meaningful and respectful way, as well as to ensure that our research, information, education and social development activities both respond to the needs of, and have an impact upon, the advocacy and self-advocacy movement.

I would like here to share some of our efforts to include people with an intellectual disability in the work we do and ensure that we remain accountable to people with disabilities.

The Roeher Institute

For a number of reasons, The Roeher Institute finds itself in an interesting position in the worlds of research, information and social development.

First, it openly declares a bias. It does not claim to be 'neutral' in terms of how it approaches its analyses of social and economic policies. The mandate of the Institute is to try to understand social policy in terms of its impact on a sector of the population which, due to the very structure of society, is largely excluded and marginalised. In its policy work the Institute is committed to recommending changes that would eliminate structural barriers to the full participation of people with disabilities as citizens. Similarly, in terms of information gathering and dissemination, The Roeher Institute has concentrated on material that supports the inclusion of people with disabilities in society. It is unlikely, for example, that one would find an extensive collection of material on curricula for segregated classes in The Roeher Institute's library (whereas there is a considerable volume of material on inclusionary educational practice). In the same way, in the delivery of our training and social development initiatives, participants are challenged to examine their understanding of what it means to have a disability and to think about the implications of viewing disability as a result of social/economic conditions rather than an individual's physiological make-up.

In all of its work The Roeher Institute strives to be accountable to the disability community and to involve people with disabilities in a substantive and meaningful way.

The Institute is a non-profit organisation which relies almost entirely upon contracts and grants to conduct its work. (Regrettably, there is no endowment from which to draw the resources to undertake projects.) Like many organisations in the not-for-profit sector, the Institute must constantly be creative in terms of balancing its own agenda (as a research institute with an interest in 'social change') with the interest of a broad range of funding sources. Sometimes there is a happy compatibility of interests between what The Roeher Institute sees as critically important and what funding agencies (including federal and provincial ministries, foundations and other private or public sector organisations) want to fund. In these instances there may very well be agreement from the outset that research (or information, or training initiatives) must be designed to ensure accountability to the disability community. These projects may include the active involvement of people with intellectual disabilities in various capacities. It is possible to conceptualise and carry out a project in such a way as to maximise the involvement of people who have been so labelled.

In other cases, however, participatory research or consumer involvement may not be high on the funding agencies' agenda. Funders may not immediately perceive the need for a design and implementation plan that maximises the involvement of people who have been labelled. In these instances The Roeher Institute plays an important role in trying to persuade funders to see the benefits of doing so, and thereby often succeeds in influencing the direction of their research agenda or how the research is conceived.

However, it would be naive to suggest that social policy research is not subject to the vagaries of the marketplace. Funding for social policy research of a certain kind is scarce; efficiency and high levels of productivity may make the difference between being awarded a contract or not. This situation is often not particularly hospitable to people who may operate at a slower pace, or require supports of various kinds, or bring with them a skill set that does not include high degrees of efficiency or productivity.

Given this context, and a commitment to including people with disabilities in the 'doing' of its work, The Roeher Institute faces a unique set of challenges. The focus of attention in our research involves examining policy issues with a view to their impact on people with a disability. But it is also extremely important to ensure that people with disabilities actively participate in our work, not simply as subjects but as agents. In all of our work it is critical that we remain accountable to the broader community of people with disabilities, meaning that we must both look to the community for direction as well as ensure that our research findings are accessible to them.

In much of the work undertaken by the Institute mechanisms are in place to draw on the expertise and knowledge of broad networks of people with disabilities and their families. Although we are not always successful in doing so, considerable attention is paid to making this involvement meaningful. The dangers of tokenism - inviting the participation of people simply because they have a disability in order to lend 'legitimacy' to a particular project - is real.

I would like to describe several of the mechanisms in place to help ensure that our work is connected to, and arising out of, the experiences and needs of people with disabilities and their families, as well as ways in which we have been striving to communicate our research findings in an accessible manner.

Board of Directors

The Roeher Institute's Board of Directors is made up of people from a wide variety of backgrounds. Currently six of the Board members are also on the Board of Directors of CACL. The presence of CACL members on our Board, in addition to disability rights advocates who may or may not have an affiliation to CACL, is an important mechanism for ensuring accountability and responsiveness to the disability movement, to individuals with disabilities and their families.

The diversity of the composition of the Board (including academics and other professionals, members of the not-for-profit sector, business people, disability rights advocates and family members) is a great strength. However, it is also an ongoing challenge to ensure that Board meetings are conducted in a manner that encourages the participation of people who have been labelled intellectually disabled. Given the infrequency of these meetings (2-3 times per year), these meetings can be very intense and involve discussions about complex issues.

To ensure inclusiveness, Board members (and staff) have to be conscious of the language they use and the difficulties some individuals may have in following, and in contributing to, discussions of a theoretical or abstract nature. Practically, this means that Board members must, on occasion, be reminded to slow down and to use more plain language. This is an ongoing process in which the Chair, in particular, plays an important role in pacing the discussions, clarifying complex issues and encouraging and facilitating the participation of all.

Advisory Committees

For every one of our research projects, we work with an advisory committee drawn from a variety of circles and including social policy analysts, representatives from the disability community and representatives from appropriate sectors depending on the nature of the study (for example, education, social services, government, private sector, etc.).

Advisory committees meet on several occasions during the course of the research, advising on the methodology as well as reviewing and commenting on preliminary findings. The presence of representatives from the disability community is critical to ensuring that the research is responding to, and addressing, the needs of people with disabilities. The advisory committees also provide an important opportunity for the concerns and issues of people with disabilities to be heard and understood by all members of the committee, and play an important role in bringing disability issues into relief in the broader research and policy community.

Straightforward 'Guides to Issues'

In recent years we have conducted a number of studies on issues such as income security, education and literacy, employment, new technologies, violence and abuse. These studies generally involve a combination of analysis of social policy, qualitative research (including interviews with various stakeholders), statistical analysis and recommendations for policy change. The reports that result from these studies tend to be text-heavy, generally book length and not very accessible to people with limited literacy skills.

It became apparent to us that we needed to develop an alternative format for people for whom the information in our reports and books was not accessible because they were unable to read, or because there was simply too much text. We began what was to become a series of straightforward 'Guides to issues', called the *Rights, Justice, Power* series.

Our first study on the issue of sexual abuse, called *Vulnerable: Sexual Abuse and People with an Intellectual Handicap,* was published as a 115 page book. Taking the main ideas out of that research, we subsequently published an accessible version called *The Right to Control What Happens to Your Body: A Straightforward Guide to Issues of Sexuality and Sexual Abuse.*

Along with our study, *Literacy and Labels: A Look at Literacy Policy and People with Mental Handicaps*, we published a plain language edition, called *The Right to Read and Write: A Straightforward Guide to Literacy and People with a Mental Handicap in Canada*.

A parallel edition to our policy study called *Income Insecurity: The Disability Income System in Canada* is the plain language book, *The Right to Have Enough Money: A Straightforward Guide to the Disability Income System in Canada.*

After publishing *On Target? Canada's Employment-Related Programs for Persons with Disabilities* we came out with *The Right to Have a Job: A Straightforward Guide to Canada's Employment-Related Program for Persons with Disabilities*.

The *Rights, Justice, Power* project was co-managed by a woman who has been labelled intellectually disabled. She worked with our staff to bring together teams of advisers, primarily other self-advocates, to determine both the format and the content of each of these publications. We began with a draft plain language version and met on a number of occasions with the advisory teams to ensure that the language was appropriate, that we were conveying the ideas in an accessible fashion and also that the information being conveyed was useful and helpful. Adaptations to content were made when needed. (For example, we were advised to include information about sexuality in the plain language version of *Vulnerable* so that people would understand what we meant by sexual abuse; we produced a plain language book on human rights, even though we had not produced a research study in this area).

The advisory committees were also able to provide direction with respect to the format and look of the documents. We needed to find a way to convey complex policy issues that have concrete implications for people with disabilities. Together we came up with a format that allowed us to include images - photographs with dialogue - that bring the issues alive and make them real. The photographs and dialogue make it possible to present the information and initiate discussions with individuals who may not be able to read or are just learning how to read. The result is a series of straightforward guides dealing with complex issues in a highly accessible format that are not only being used by self-advocates, but are also being used in literacy programmes across the country.

We have recently published several other plain language publications: *Out of Harm's Way: A Safety Kit for People with Disabilities who Feel Unsafe and Want to Do Something About It; A Straightforward Guide to the Internet;* and *The Power of Language* (workshops on plain language). While the format of these books is somewhat different from that of the

Rights, Justice, Power series, the process for developing them was similar. In each case, the process involved the following:

- the identification of a need for information, based on research findings, training initiatives and needs identified by CACL or by The Roeher Institute Board of Directors

- the development of an advisory committee of self-advocates and, when appropriate, their advisers

- presentation of drafts of material for discussion with the advisory committee

- revisions to drafts, and presentation of revised drafts for comment

- publication and distribution of the books.

Seeking Consent to Participate in Research

In conducting our research we have, on numerous occasions, faced the dilemma of how to respectfully obtain the consent to be interviewed from people whose ability to make an informed decision could be questioned. The research industry tends to label many people with intellectual disabilities in a way that undermines their status, by establishing guidelines for consent that require that they be able to meet traditional standards for 'competency'; failing that, a third party can consent on their behalf. This creates an ethical dilemma for an organisation whose research mandate is to promote the human rights of people with disabilities. The traditional model draws on an understanding of the self that views competence as the pre-requisite for exercising self-determination. In contrast to the traditional approach that labels people as competent (or incompetent), we have developed an alternative model that builds on the recognition that self-determination is exercised in relationship with others.

This model, the Supported Decision-Making model, presumes that each adult participant is competent; that any needs for decision-making support in order to evaluate the risks and benefits of participating in a research project are acknowledged and accommodated; and that the individual and the person providing the decision-making support review information about the proposed research and together determine whether or not the individual will consent to participate.

The development of this model means that people with intellectual disabilities, whose competence is often called into question, can participate in most of our research projects, without having to be declared 'competent' or 'incompetent', and without reinforcing or contributing to the labelling of people. Consent for participation is now respectfully obtained using the Supported Decision-Making model.

While these examples suggest important successes, how we ensure the respectful and meaningful involvement and participation of people with an intellectual disability in our work is an ongoing issue. We will continue to struggle to make our Board meeting and the meetings of our research advisory committees more accessible and inclusive. Ensuring that people with disabilities inform the research agenda, participate in the research, and have access to the knowledge that is created through the research, is fundamental to what we do. We are committed to finding new and creative ways to make it happen.

References

The Roeher Institute (1988) *Vulnerable: Sexual abuse and people with an intellectual handicap*. Toronto: The Roeher Institute

The Roeher Institute (1989) *Literacy and Labels: A look at literacy policy and people with mental handicaps. Income Security: the disability income system in Canada*. Toronto: The Roeher Institute.

The Roeher Institute (1993) *On Target? Canada's Employment-related Programs for Person's with Disabilities*. Toronto: The Roeher Institute.

Plain Language publications produced by The Roeher Institute

The Right to Have Enough Money: A Straightforward Guide to the Disability Income System in Canada. (1990)

The Right to Read and Write: A Straightforward Guide to Literacy and people with a Mental Handicap in Canada. (1990)

The Right to Control what Happens to Your Body: A Straightforward Guide to Issues of Sexuality and Sexual Abuse. (1991)

The Right to Fair and Equal Treatment: A Straightforward Guide to the Canadian Human Rights Act. (1991)

The Right to Have a Job: A Straightforward Guide to Canada's Employment-Related Programs for Persons with Disabilities. (1994)

Just Technology?' Plain Language Summary of 'Just Technology?' From Principles to Practice in Bio-Ethical Issues. (1995

Out of Harm's Way: A Safety Kit for People with Disabilities who Feel Unsafe and Want to Do Something About It. (1997)

The Power of Language. (Workbook, Handbook and Facilitator's Guide on Plain Language Writing.) (1997)

A Straightforward Guide to the Internet. (1997)

Miriam Ticoll has been involved in the information field for the past two decades. Over the past decade she has been committed to finding innovative ways to ensure that people with disabilities have access to information and are involved in knowledge creation. Her work at The Roeher Institute includes directing the activities of an international clearing house and information service on disability issues. She also has extensive involvement in the research, training and publishing activities of the Institute, with particular interest in issues pertaining to violence and to literacy.

Contact address
> The Roeher Institute
> Kinsmen Building, York University
> 4700 Keele Street
> North York
> Ontario M3J 1PS,
> Canada

7 Learning for Change?
Participation and Empowerment through Continuing Education for Adults with Learning Difficulties

Jeannie Sutcliffe and Richard West

We need to think about the learning 'have nots'…we have been working with a system based on hierarchy, exclusion and failure and we must change this.
(Professor Bob Fryer, Chair of the National Advisory Group for Continuing Education and Lifelong Learning, speaking at a NIACE conference, December 1997)

Training for Change: A New Course in Development

Adults with learning difficulties are increasingly being asked to do training in health, social services and other settings. They are often asked to train staff, and sometimes users, in relation to issues affecting the lives of people with learning difficulties, such as rights or self-advocacy. There is a gap in existing resources in terms of materials to support the development of training skills for people with learning difficulties. NIACE (the national organisation for adult learning) is working with CHANGE (an organisation run by disabled people) to produce a pack to support adults with learning difficulties who want to be trainers. The pack has been developed with contributions from people with learning difficulties who work at CHANGE and who have offered their perspectives from the viewpoint of, for example, also being black, deaf or having mental health difficulties. CHANGE campaigns for equal rights and equal access for all people with learning disabilities, including people who are also deaf and/or blind, who are often left out of services. People with learning difficulties at

CHANGE do training and consultancy work and are employed as project workers and volunteer workers.

The steering group for the 'Training for Change' project includes other people with learning difficulties who have experience of training. This has added a valuable contribution to the work. Steering group minutes are in simple language and illustrated, which makes it easier for everyone!

The pack has been funded by the Department of Health. It covers topics ranging from being in a group and going to meetings, to doing a talk or presentation. The modules are arranged as follows:

Unit title	Modules in pack covered
Training and me	• Introducing training (via the video) • Being in a group • 'I can and I want to' self assessment
Making a start	• Going to a meeting • Let's relax • Presenting ourselves
Rights and choices	• Our rights • Make it fair • Saying no
Planning and doing training	• Planning • Ways of teaching • Giving a talk • How did it go?
Finding things to help with training	• Resources • Doing your own research • Organising yourself

The pack and course are designed for people with learning difficulties who already have an understanding of self-advocacy. The pack uses clear language and is fully illustrated. There are hand-outs, group work and individual work, backed up by a checklist and suggestions for resources (see samples on p.'s. 104 and 105).

We realised that for the many people with learning difficulties who have little or no reading ability, producing text-based materials, even illustrated ones, would be limiting. In order to make the pack as accessible as possible, a video and an audio-tape are being made in collaboration with Mental Health Media, with additional funding from the National Lottery Charities Board. People with learning difficulties were involved in interviewing prospective video makers, and will also be active partners in making the video. At the time of writing the video outline is just being planned. The video will show different examples of training in action, before homing in on one example of training from start to finish. It will have themes which tie in to the pack contents. We hope it will be good fun to watch, as well as educational!

A submission is being made to the National Open College Network to have the course accredited. This will be done at a national level, so that any Open College will be able to validate the course. Staff can apply to their nearest Open College Network organisation to run the course with accreditation. The course will be accredited at two levels: Entry Level (designed for students who require an intensive level of support) and Level One (which can be undertaken by students who can work more independently). As an accredited vocational course at Level One, it would then be eligible for inclusion in the Department for Education and Employment list of approved courses. This would in turn make the course eligible for Further Education Funding Council funding. The course is designed to be co-tutored by people with learning difficulties who have the relevant experience or else who have successfully done the course.

The pack was piloted by about 20 places in the summer of 1997, including colleges, local education authorities, social services departments and others.

Jeannie Sutcliffe and Richard West

SAMPLE PAGES FROM 'TRAINING FOR CHANGE' PACK

In the group

Going to a meeting

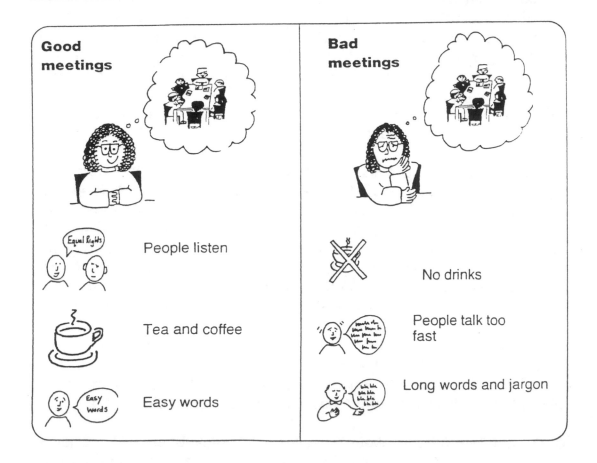

Good meetings

People listen

Tea and coffee

Easy words

Bad meetings

No drinks

People talk too fast

Long words and jargon

You have talked as a group about what makes meetings good and bad for everyone.

Now think about what **YOU** need to make meetings work for you.

Here are some ideas of things that people have asked for...

Sign Language Interpreter

Access for people who use wheelchairs

Notes on tape or in Braille

Special diet

What do you need?
Write it down (with help if you need) or put it on tape.

The full pack, with video and audio-tape and the option of Open College Network accreditation, will be launched in November 1998. It can either be used as a course in its entirety or used in a 'pick and mix' way to dip into. NIACE and CHANGE hope that it will be a tool for change, which will support self-advocacy and the empowerment of adults with learning difficulties. Richard West from CHANGE describes why he became involved and what his hopes are for the course:

My name is Richard West. I am a black deaf person with learning disabilities and I work as a trainer/consultant and campaigns officer in CHANGE. All the consultants in CHANGE have learning disabilities and some of us are deaf and blind too. We run workshops all round the country for people with learning disabilities and staff. We support people with learning disabilities to speak out for their rights to good services.

It is important that trainers are people with disabilities because we can give other people with learning disabilities confidence. People with learning disabilities know best about services and the problems disabled people may have.

If people with learning disabilities are interested in how to be a trainer this course will support them. It is important the course is accessible so people with learning disabilities can also teach on the course. I feel very pleased the course information is easy to read with pictures for people with learning disabilities. After all, I myself am a person with learning disabilities.

It is very important that people with learning disabilities have the opportunity to go to college and get a qualification as this gives us confidence, more power and equal rights. Not many people with learning disabilities have the chance to do this at the moment. We need a strong voice to train staff and each other to speak up for our rights.

We hope this course, which people with learning disabilities have helped to develop, using our own experiences as trainers, will be positive. We hope it will help people with learning disabilities to improve their lives, get proper jobs and have more power in life. This is the last point I want to make to you…. Give people with learning disabilities more power. We have power in our rights and we have the right to get good training, qualifications and proper jobs.

Current Issues

So, what are the main issues in continuing education for adults with learning difficulties? What major developments have had an impact in recent years? What direction are services in colleges and adult education centres taking particularly in relation to self-advocacy and empowerment? Who participates in learning and who misses out?

Recent developments

The two most significant developments in the 1990s are the Further and Higher Education Act (1992) and the publication of *Inclusive Learning* (HMSO, 1996), the report of the Further Education Funding Council's committee on learning difficulties and/or disabilities.

The Further and Higher Education Act (1992) made colleges in England and Wales independent of local authority control. The Further Education Funding Council (FEFC) was set up following the Act. It funds colleges to run courses listed under a part of the Further and Higher Education Act (1992) called Schedule 2. This list includes courses in independent living and communication skills for adults with learning difficulties. Progression to other Schedule 2 courses (for example, vocational and academic qualifications, literacy and numeracy) is required. Local education authorities can also offer Schedule 2 courses funded by the FEFC, but they have a duty to provide other sorts of courses too, for example, non-vocational courses such as holiday French or cake decorating. There has been a fierce debate about the vocational/non-vocational divide. For example, a business woman may be learning basic French for work purposes, while some people start out decorating cakes as a hobby and then go on to do it professionally.

Mary goes to a number of part-time courses run by the local education authority. These include yoga, cookery and basic skills. She says: 'It gets me out of the house and I learn something new.'

Carl goes to college part-time to do a vocational motor vehicle maintenance course. He has a learning support worker to help him in the workshop when needed. His college has a tradition of people with severe learning difficulties joining in with regular classes with highly trained support staff, who work one to one.

In response to concerns from practitioners about the impact of the Further and Higher Education Act (1992), the National Institute of Adult Continuing Education (NIACE) carried out research supported by the Joseph Rowntree Foundation to explore the impact of the changes specifically on adults with learning difficulties. The work was carried out in partnership with the Norah Fry Research Centre at the University of Bristol. *Still A Chance to Learn?* (Macadam and Sutcliffe, 1996) details the full findings. In summary, the research found that the curriculum offered had narrowed as people in colleges and local education authorities had sought to satisfy the Further Education Funding Council's funding criteria. An increase in life skills and vocational courses was reported, with the loss of some non-vocational (i.e. not directly job related) courses such as music, art and a women's group. Students with learning difficulties told NIACE how upset they felt: 'We just want our courses back!'

The cuts to opportunities are a matter of ongoing concern, as non-vocational courses are an important part of the curriculum. NIACE has always argued in favour of the widest possible range of courses being offered. At the same time, social services day services are increasingly turning to education as part of a package of alternatives to traditional day centre provision. With the emphasis on progression and accreditation for Further Education Funding Council funded courses, there are some tensions in providing for adults with learning difficulties, who tend to make slower progress in their learning. Our research showed that practitioners feared that the drive towards accreditation would exclude the more vulnerable groups of learners. *Still A Chance To Learn?* found that local education authorities were more likely than individual colleges to be working with health and social services.

The funding mechanism which was implemented following the Further and Higher Education Act (1992) made it possible for funding to be individualised. There has been an increase in integrated learning, with people with learning difficulties learning alongside non-disabled students.

Inclusive Learning (1996) was the final report of the Further Education Funding Council's learning difficulties and/or disabilities committee, chaired by Professor John Tomlinson. This long, detailed report had many recommendations for improving the quality of teaching and learning for adults with learning difficulties and/or disabilities. A consultation exercise by the FEFC in 1997 showed widespread support for the major recommendations in the report. Consequently, the Further Education Funding Council set up an inclusive learning steering group to seek to implement these and/or consider how to take them further. The FEFC condensed the recommendations down to 60 key ones, including a proposal to develop provision for people with profound and multiple learning difficulties in colleges. This group was one of three highlighted by the report as being under-represented in provision.

Self-advocacy

Learning to make choices and decisions is a fundamental part of speaking up. In the book *Self-advocacy and adults with learning difficulties* (Sutcliffe and Simons, 1993), three key themes recur:

- Self-advocacy is complex and diverse. There are many forms of self-advocacy operating in a wide range of contexts, and there is no 'right' kind of self-advocacy. A number of self-advocacy groups have their origins in adult and further education, even if they are now independent.

- Self-advocacy takes time and more time. Individuals and groups need to develop at their own pace, which often takes longer than professionals anticipate. This point is potentially difficult in relation to the current further education funding system, with its new emphasis on progression and accreditation.

- Self-advocacy needs resources. Securing funds whilst trying to remain independent from service providers is a tension. For example, one People First group has met for years under the auspices of the adult education service. It has finally been able to make the break to be independent, but there are now anxieties about premises, support staff and fund-raising.

Some areas have had a long standing commitment to self-advocacy. In Cardiff, the local education authority (in collaboration with the social services department) offers self-advocacy courses delivered as a part of the community education programme for over 100 adults, with transport provided. An inter-agency training programme has been devised and accredited by the Welsh Joint Education Committee. People can progress to join local People First (self-advocacy) groups. Provision at this level and of this nature is still rare. The *Inclusive Learning* report recommends that more self-advocacy courses should be developed, as does the Mental Health Foundation in their publication *Building Expectations* (1996). It will be important to press for these recommendations on self-advocacy courses to be implemented.

Who participates and who misses out?

At the time of the *Still A Chance to Learn?* survey, adults with moderate learning difficulties were receiving a thriving service with increased numbers attending education, but there were concerns about marginalised groups, such as older adults and those with profound and multiple learning difficulties. As a result, NIACE (with support from the Joseph Rowntree Foundation) is now undertaking the project *All Things Being Equal?*, to explore practice in relation to marginalised groups of adults with learning difficulties in continuing education. Early findings indicate that there is little imaginative provision (for example, for black adults with learning difficulties or for older adults with learning difficulties) and that which does exist is very fragile. For example, one tutor running a black arts group for adults with learning difficulties has to constantly justify why the group exists. It is the only group of its kind in a large city. Equally, the perception of developing educational provision for older adults was very limited in many places. One respondent asked: 'Do you mean people over 27?' The project is currently documenting examples of provision which are rare but important, such as a course for deaf adults with learning difficulties taught by deaf tutors.

There is evidence from *Still A Chance To Learn?* (Macadam and Sutcliffe,1996) and from *Mapping Provision* (Insitute for Employment Studies,1997) to indicate that adults with learning difficulties are more likely to be under-represented in education if they are women, from black or minority ethnic groups or older adults. In addition, those with profound/multiple learning difficulties tend to miss out, and this is one of the groups highlighted by the *Inclusive Learning* report as being under-represented. There are also difficulties in accessing education for people who have the dual label of learning difficulties and mental health difficulties and for those described as having challenging behaviour. There is evidence that colleges could be catering for twice as many disabled students as they actually take (Institute for Employment Studies, 1997).

In Conclusion: A New Tomorrow?

Professor John Tomlinson, speaking at a NIACE conference in November 1997, declared that he felt optimistic that change was in progress in relation to the future of education for people with learning difficulties and/or disabilities. Certainly, there have been significant developments recently which should back up the key recommendations in *Inclusive Learning*. The report *Learning Works* from the FEFC clearly argues the case for wider participation (Kennedy, 1997). Social exclusion is a key government concern; it is also firmly on the agenda of the National Advisory Group on Continuing Education and Lifelong Learning (NAGCELL). Adults with learning difficulties are given several specific mentions as an under-represented group in the first NAGCELL report, *Learning for the Twenty-First Century* (Fryer, 1997).

In addition, NIACE has recently been awarded a two year National Lottery Charities Board grant to produce a charter by/for adults with learning difficulties about what they want from learning. This ten point charter will be produced in an accessible format and will be distributed to all colleges, local education authorities and self-advocacy groups in the UK. There will also be a booklet expanding on the charter, which will provide a framework for quality standards in learning, as defined by users. We hope that this might also provide current examples of how self-advocacy, participation and empowerment can be embedded as a part of college and adult education life.

These initiatives all give us hope that things will get better. As we head towards the year 2000, it is clear that continuing education for adults with learning difficulties still has plenty of scope for development. Until colleges and adult education services cater for all students with learning difficulties, regardless of race, gender and disability, how can we claim to be living in an inclusive society?

Acknowledgements

Illustrations are by Clare Davis.

References

Fryer, R.H. (1997) *Learning for the Twenty First Century. (*First report of the National Advisory Group for Continuing Education and Lifelong Learning.) Sudbury, Suffolk: Department for Education & Employment.

Institute for Employment Studies (1997) *Mapping Provision: Report prepared by the Institute for Employment Studies.* London: The Stationery Office.

Kennedy, H. QC (1997) *Learning Works: Widening Participation in Further Education.* Coventry: FEFC.

Learning Difficulties & Disabilities Committee (1996) *Inclusive Learning: Report of the Learning Difficulties & Disabilities Committee.* London: The Stationery Office.

Macadam, M. and Sutcliffe, J. (1996) *Still A Chance To Learn? A report of a project on the impact of the Further & Higher Education Act (1992) on education for adults with learning difficulties.* Leicester: NIACE.

The Mental Health Foundation (1996) *Building Expectations: Opportunities & Services for People with a Learning Disability.* London: The Mental Health Foundation.

NIACE in collaboration with CHANGE (1998) *Training for Change: A pack to support adults with learning difficulties to become trainers.* Leicester: NIACE.

Sutcliffe, J. and Jacobsen, Y. (1998) *All Things Being Equal? Report of a project on equal opportunities in relation to continuing education for adults with learning difficulties.* Leicester: NIACE.

Sutcliffe, J. and Simons, K. (1993) *Self-advocacy and adults with learning difficulties.* Leicester: NIACE.

Jeannie Sutcliffe has worked as a development officer for the National Institute of Adult Continuing Education (NIACE) since 1988. Before that, she taught in adult and further education in Essex and Bedfordshire. She has produced a number of books and packs for NIACE in relation to continuing education for adults with learning difficulties, including titles on basic skills, integration and self-advocacy.

Richard West has worked for CHANGE since early 1994. He is a consultant and campaign worker with learning disabilities. Richard has worked on a number of different projects for CHANGE. One of his main interest is making information accessible to people with learning difficulties. Richard is currently working with London Transport and the Department of Transport to make the tube and bus systems accessible by using pictures and symbols at stations and on maps . He is also advising the British Museum about accessible information. Richard was supported by colleagues at CHANGE to make his contribution to the chapter for this book.

Contact addresses

Jeannie Sutcliffe
NIACE
21 De Montfort Street
Leicester LE1 7GE
England

Richard West
CHANGE
1st Floor, 69-85 Old Street
London EC1V 9HY
Tel: 0171 490 2668
Minicom: 0171 490 3483
E-mail: contact@changeuk.demon.co.uk

8 Reclaiming Our Past
Empowerment through Oral History and Personal Stories

Dorothy Atkinson

Introduction

You've got something to show for your life. You've got something so that you can say, 'That's what happened to me'. It will keep history in my mind for years to come, what's happened to me and a lot of others like me.

This is Mabel Cooper speaking about her life story, and why it matters. Her life story is no 'ordinary' story; it takes its readers into a separate and segregated world of children's homes and long-stay institutions. The process of telling the story was important to Mabel in making sense of history - not just her own personal history ('what's happened to me') but the history of many thousands of people who, like herself, were labelled and excluded from everyday life. The end-product, the written narrative, is 'something to show' for a life lived to a large extent in a separate world.

Although she does not use the word, Mabel is talking about empowerment - the gaining of power through knowledge and understanding. In telling her story, Mabel has developed an historical awareness of her own situation and the situation of others (Freire, 1986). This has proved empowering and has led to a quest on her part to know more; to find out about her life from documentary sources, and to challenge past language, labels, assumptions and practices. Her life story, as she and I first wrote it, has turned out to be only the first volume in a two volume (at least) series in which we are now engaged. If the process is empowering, the product - the book - represents empowerment. It has enabled Mabel to represent herself through her autobiography and, thereby, to own and control the story of her life (Adams, 1996; Jack, 1995). In so doing, she has come to understand oppression and to challenge it (Ward and Mullender, 1991), and has confirmed her status as a 'border crosser' from the excluded world into the heart of mainstream society (Borland and Ramcharan, 1997; Rolph, 1997).

This chapter is about the telling and recording of life stories. It refers to the full life story - or autobiography - which Mabel is working on (and which we return to later) but it also looks at oral history as a means by which the stories of people with learning difficulties come to be told. Oral history is a way of reconstructing the past through people's spoken memories of the time. It enables people to speak about their own lives so that their personal histories are recorded, and valued. When several individual histories are brought together they begin to tell more than personal stories; they begin to reveal a shared history of the time.

Empowerment through Oral History

Why oral history?

> *We had a back-to-back house with a cellar and gas lights. We*
> *had a coal fire and a coal hole.*

These sound like ordinary memories of northern working class life in the earlier years of this century. In a sense they are, but they were spoken by a man with learning difficulties whose life in later years turned out to be far from ordinary. They were spoken by Brian Sutcliffe, a member of the oral history group which I set up to enable people to tell their stories. Brian's memories of childhood and schooldays at least have elements in common with other people's memories, even if his later experiences were quite different. The use of oral history with people with learning difficulties makes it possible to draw out the commonalities as well as the differences between their lives and ours.

There are, however, very few examples of oral history in the learning disability field. This is hardly surprising. Variously seen as threats to society, the perpetrators of numerous social ills or as impaired or otherwise afflicted victims, people with learning difficulties have often led segregated lives in special educational and residential institutions. Their symbolic, and actual exclusion, from ordinary, everyday life has meant that they have become invisible (Bornat, 1992). Their voices were rarely heard because, until recently, few people thought they had anything of value to say. It is important now to begin to redress this balance. The use of oral history is one means of achieving that goal.

In my *Past Times* oral history project, I used reminiscence and recall to enable a group of people with learning difficulties to find a voice (Atkinson, 1997). In so doing, the project built on the work of two other similar ventures. The first of these was *Know Me As I Am* (Atkinson and Williams, 1990) an anthology of first-hand accounts by people with learning difficulties about their lives and experiences. These accounts gave a detailed and rounded picture of diverse people with distinctive pasts. A second influential example of the use of oral history with people with learning difficulties is the work of Potts and Fido (1991). Through individual interviews with 17 past and present older residents, they co-constructed an oral history of a long-stay institution in the north of England.

In the two earlier projects, the focus on remembered pasts acted as an important antidote to the more usual portrayals of people with learning difficulties which draw on, for example, documented accounts of institutional life or are based on assessments or scales which measure individual deficits or problems. Oral history redresses the balance. It enables people to tell their story in their own words, and to be seen, and to see themselves, as survivors rather than victims. In their own accounts, people emerge not as people deficient in skills, or lacking the correct social behaviour, but as individuals with a personal history, a culture, a class, a gender, as well as an impairment (Atkinson and Williams, 1990, p.8).

The Past Times Project

The Past Times project involved a group of people with learning difficulties recalling, and talking about, their past lives. The group consisted of nine people; seven men and two women. Their ages ranged from 57 to 77, with most people being in their late 60s or early 70s. Prospective members were approached, and invited to join, via the staff of the special residential and day settings where they were then service users. The group meetings were held at first weekly, then later fortnightly. They lasted for an hour and, with permission, were tape recorded and transcribed. The group was initially set up by me as a modest project which would run for six weeks or so but, in fact, it continued to meet over a period of two years. This reflects both the enjoyment and the growing sense of self which this project, much to my surprise, brought to its members. The group's life was extended because it became apparent that this was indeed a forum where experiences could be remembered, re-lived and shared.

I set the project up with two aims in mind. The first aim was to provide the time and space (the forum) where people could tell their stories. The idea was to use the oral history techniques of recall and reminiscence to enable group members to recount and explore their individual histories. The second aim built on the first: to use these personal accounts to begin to construct a more collective historical account of the policy and provision for people with learning difficulties during this century. This was intended to be history 'from below' (Humphries, 1984) and was to be, if possible, a joint effort or co-construction of the past.

The Past Times project used a group setting, and relied on group meetings throughout its two years of life. I chose a group setting for two reasons: to provide a supportive and friendly atmosphere where (sometimes) painful memories could be shared; and to provide a setting where one person's memories of past events would spark off memories in other people. The group format in the end worked quite well in that the group eventually became that supportive-but-stimulating environment which I had envisaged. But it took time, and practice, to reach that point. Early group meetings were characterised at times by silence and, at other times, by anarchic cross-talking and multiple side conversations. Some members loved to hold the floor and tell long stories; others sat quietly, venturing little. Various memory triggers were used, ranging from the simple, 'Do you remember ...?' to the use of professionally produced reminiscence slides and tapes, and our own authentic cigarette cards, photographs and other memorabilia of the time. (A fuller account of the project is available elsewhere: see, for example, Atkinson, 1997.)

Running the group was never easy. There were problems of communication throughout our meetings, as it was often difficult for me to understand the words and content of many of the contributions. This often still applied later on when I replayed the tapes at home. One or two staff members from the day and residential services, who knew group members well, joined in the meetings and helped where they could with translation and interpretation. Thus we struggled, together, to hear and be heard, for a whole year. At that point we took a break from meetings, to give me the opportunity to compile the numerous fragments and vignettes from the (by now) large pile of transcripts into a booklet which I entitled *Past Times*.

This booklet was, as it turned out, the first of a series of versions of 'our book' (as group members preferred to a call it). A series of readings from *Past Times,* over a period of many weeks, triggered off more and deeper memories. A second draft was compiled which incorporated these new accounts. Again, I proceeded on a series of readings from the expanded version and, again, more memories emerged. Thus a third and final version of *Past Times* was produced, reflecting the group's wish that we should produce a 'bigger and better' book rather than just a booklet (Atkinson, 1993). Presumably the process of readings-and-amendments could have continued indefinitely with the book continuing to grow. Indeed it seemed at the time that group members would have preferred to go on forever rather than, after two years, being persuaded to stop.

The *Past Times* Book

The group's written account, *Past Times*, was of immense importance to its members. As people with learning difficulties they had had restricted access to the written word. Yet they clearly recognised its value as a means of influencing opinion and shaping attitudes. They wanted their work to be in print because they wanted other people to know about them and their lives. They also saw the written word as authoritative. Their experiences were, it seemed, validated through being written down.

The book has proved to be of interest to people beyond its own contributors, and their immediate circle of families and friends. This is because it offers a rich compilation of individual and shared memories. Some accounts of childhood and schooldays were, as I suggested earlier, quite ordinary for their time and place. The quotation from Brian, earlier, is typical of many such memories. But sooner or later, each contributor's life had changed as they had become users of separate, or segregated, services. For some, like Margaret Day, this happened in childhood, as the following extract illustrates:

> *When I was a little girl I was put away. I was fourteen and a half. I went to Cell Barnes to live because they said I was backward. My dad refused to sign the papers for me to go, but the police came and said he would go to prison if he didn't. I cried when I had to go with the Welfare Officer.*

The book, *Past Times,* includes shared memories of hospital life. These afford us glimpses into a hidden world hitherto described primarily in formal documents. In the following extract, George Coley recalls a well-remembered character from years ago:

> *I don't know if Bert still remembers Lewis? He was a Charge Nurse. He used to have three stripes on each arm and three pips on the top of his jacket. And first thing in the morning you knew he was about. If you said anything, and he went like that [raises his arm], you knew what he meant. Bed!*

The Outcome of the Project

The project was empowering for those involved. Although I had set up the oral history project, and had run it, nevertheless the participants were able to use the situation to tell their own individual and linked stories, using my research skills. They had harnessed my skills of listening, recording, transcribing and editing to work on their 'bigger and better' version of *Past Times* . The group members thus showed research awareness, as well as historical awareness, and had made the first step towards changing the classic power relationship between researcher and subjects which still characterises most research. Having been invited to be participants in my research project, these nine people with learning difficulties subsequently became active shapers of that research agenda. This was an empowering process and led to a shift towards a more 'emancipatory research' (Zarb, 1992).

Empowerment through Autobiography

Why autobiography?

The ultimate personal story is, of course, the autobiography. Usually the preserve of the rich and famous the autobiography, at least in principle, offers the possibility to people with learning difficulties of self-representation - another means by which people's voices can be heard. It is not easy to produce one's autobiography without help; and this applies to the rich and famous as well as people with learning difficulties. Most people need a collaborator, even a ghost writer, but an autobiographer with learning difficulties is likely to need 'a facilitator, an interpreter and a scribe' if the story is to be written at all (Atkinson and Walmsley, forthcoming).

It is only in recent years that people with learning difficulties have begun to represent themselves. This has occurred partly through self-advocacy, where people have begun to 'speak up' on their own behalf, but also through the growing popularity of the autobiography or life story. Although becoming more popular there are still relatively few published autobiographies of people with learning difficulties. One of the best known is Joey Deacon's story, *Tongue Tied* (1974) which was subsequently dramatised for television. Other examples include: *The World of Nigel Hunt* (1967); *My Life Story* (1991) by Malcolm Burnside; and the one I return to below, *Mabel Cooper's Life Story* (1997).

Producing an autobiography

I want to return now to Mabel Cooper's autobiographical research and writing. My involvement in working with Mabel began when she asked me to help her write her life story. We met at her home where she talked to me about her childhood in children's homes, her subsequent move to St Lawrence's Hospital and her later life in the community, including her work in the self-advocacy movement. We tape-recorded our conversations and I later transcribed them word for word. The process was a small-scale, and individual, version of the *Past Times* project in that I prepared a more flowing narrative account from the question-and-answer transcripts, and then read the narrative back to Mabel for confirmation or amendment. The readings triggered more memories which were themselves incorporated into the developing story. The result was initially a private publication for Mabel and her friends, but subsequently the story was published in a book (Cooper, 1997).

Just as the *Past Times* project had brought in its wake greater understanding for people of their own lives and the lives of others, so the autobiographical process enabled Mabel to make sense of her life and to see it in a wider social context. In telling her story, she was not only reclaiming her own past, she was, at the same time, reflecting on the social history of learning disability in this century. The extract below, from her life story, combines personal history with period detail. Here, Mabel recalls how and why she came to leave the children's home in Bedford to move to St Lawrence's Hospital in Caterham:

> *I moved to St Lawrence's when I was seven, because they only took children what went to school in this home. And I never went to school, so I had to move. In them days they give you a test. You went to London or somewhere because they'd give you a test before they make you go anywhere. It used to be a big place, all full of offices and what-have-you. Because they said you should be able to read when you're seven or eight. I couldn't read, I hadn't been to school. That was 1952, I was seven years old. [....]*

When I first went in there, even just getting out of the car you could hear the racket. You think you're going to a madhouse. When you first went there you could hear people screaming and shouting outside. It was very noisy but I think you do get used to them after a little while because it's like everywhere that's big. If there's a lot of people you get a lot of noise, and they had like big dormitories, didn't they? (Cooper, 1997)

There is no doubt that Mabel gained historical awareness and understanding through the process of writing her autobiography - and there is no doubt that the finished product brought with it a great sense of achievement. The experience of being an autobiographer has been a rewarding one. Mabel is well aware of her role as an historical witness, a role which entails letting people know what life was like for herself and others in the past. In one of our many subsequent conversations about the meaning and significance of her autobiography, Mabel pinpointed both the sense of personal achievement it brought for her and its importance as an historical record of the past:

It's an achievement with me being in St Lawrence's for so many years, and not knowing anything else but St Lawrence's. I thought it would be nice to let people know what it was like, and to let people know how difficult it was for someone with a learning disability, and who was stuck away because of that. I thought that people outside should know these things because they're not aware of it at the moment and I think it would be nice.
(Quoted in Atkinson, Jackson and Walmsley, 1997)

The compilation of Mabel's account from memory has pinpointed gaps in her story. She was left with many unanswered questions, for example: Who was she? Who were her parents? What had become of them? Mabel's need to know has led her into a quest for documentary evidence from her own case records and from the archived records of the institutions where she spent her childhood and much of her adult life. Such a quest has seemed daunting at times, and some of the language of the past has been hurtful, but the need to know has proved a strong driving force. The quest has taken Mabel and myself to view her case notes at the offices of the Lifecare Trust (on the site of St Lawrence's), and to visit the London Metropolitan Archives and the Bedfordshire County Records Office. More visits are planned. The final outcome is intended - by Mabel - to be a revised and updated autobiography, based on documentary evidence as well as on memory. Mabel explains here what her historical research is for, and what it entails:

> *There's so much I didn't know that I'm finding out now. I went to St Lawrence's (the location of the Lifecare Trust) and I went to the archives. Some of it, like the names they called you in them days, hurt a little bit but otherwise I thought it was great. It was something I needed to find out. And going to the archives, that was great again, that was somewhere I've never been, and I enjoyed it. It would be smashing if half of this could be put in another book so it could say this is what Mabel said about this.*

Conclusion

The telling/writing of the life story can have an impact at both a personal and a social level. At a personal level, it presents the ideal opportunity for people with learning difficulties to look back at, and make sense of, their own lives. In enabling people to tell their story, in their own words, and in their own way, the act of story-telling involves them in the all-important process of life review. Making sense of a life lived is an empowering process. It makes change both possible and feasible.

At a social level, the collecting and collating of life stories can highlight the commonalities as well as the differences in people's lives and experiences - experiences which are shared with other people with learning difficulties, as well as with the rest of society. This has the potential to encourage people with learning difficulties to develop a social awareness, and understanding, of the sources and meaning of those shared experiences. It also has the potential to involve the rest of us in a greater understanding of people's lives, and to be enriched by that understanding.

Oral history and autobiography can encourage and enhance the historical awareness of people with learning difficulties. If more people become involved in the telling of their personal histories then they also become involved in the telling of history itself. Those accounts, separately and together, will help form the history of learning disability in this century. In this way, slowly but surely, it should prove possible for people with learning difficulties to reclaim their separate and joint pasts and to know, and to own, a history which is theirs. This is empowerment through knowledge. There is no better nor more enduring kind.

References

Adams, R. (1996) *Social Work and Empowerment* (Second edition). Basingstoke: Macmillan.

Atkinson, D. (1993) *Past Times*. Milton Keynes: private publication.

Atkinson, D. (1997) *An Autobiographical Approach to Learning Disability Research.* Aldershot: Ashgate.

Atkinson, D., Jackson, M. and Walmsley, J. (1997) Introduction: Methods and Themes. In Atkinson, D., Jackson, M. and Walmsley, J. (eds). *Forgotten Lives. Exploring the History of Learning Disability*. Kidderminster: BILD Publications.

Atkinson, D. and Walmsley, J. Using Auto/Biographical Approaches with People with Learning Difficulties. *Disability & Society*, (forthcoming).

Atkinson, D. and Williams, F. (1990 eds) *Know Me As I Am: An anthology of prose, poetry and art by people with learning difficulties*. London: Hodder and Stoughton.

Borland, J. and Ramcharan, P. (1997) Empowerment in Informal Settings. In Ramcharan, P., Roberts, G., Grant, G. and Borland, J. (eds). *Empowerment in Everyday Life*. London: Jessica Kingsley.

Bornat, J. (1992) The Communities of Community Publishing. *Oral History 20, (2), pp. 23-31*.

Burnside, M. (1991) *My Life Story*. Halifax: Pecket Well College.

Cooper, M. (1997) Mabel Cooper's Life Story. In Atkinson, D., Jackson, M., and Walmsley, J. (eds) *Forgotten Lives. Exploring the History of Learning Disability.* Kidderminster: BILD Publications.

Deacon, J. (1974) *Tongue Tied.* London: NSMHC.

Freire, P. (1986) *Pedagogy of the Oppressed* (Reprint). Harmondsworth: Penguin

Humphries, S. (1984) *The Handbook of Oral History: Recording Life Stories*. London: Inter-Action Trust.

Hunt, N. (1967) *The World of Nigel Hunt.* Beaconsfield: Darwen Finlayson.

Jack, R. (1995) Empowerment in Community Care. In Jack, R. (ed). *Empowerment in Community Care.* London: Chapman and Hall.

Potts, M. and Fido, R. (1991) *A Fit Person To Be Removed.* Plymouth: Northcote House.

Rolph, S. (1997) Surprise journeys and border crossings, Conference paper presented at the History of Learning Disability Conference, Open University (School of Health & Social Welfare), July 1997.

Ward, D. and Mullender, A. (1991) Empowerment and Oppression: An indissoluble pairing for contemporary social work. *Critical Social Policy,* 32, Autumn, pp. 21-30.

Zarb, G. (1992) On the road to Damascus: first steps in changing the relations of disability research production. *Disability, Handicap and Society*, 7, (2) pp. 125-138.

Dorothy Atkinson is a Senior Lecturer in the School of Health and Social Welfare at the Open University. Her background is in social work, and includes several years experience of working with people with learning difficulties. Her OU work has included co-editing the anthology *Know Me As I Am* (1990). Her current research interest is in exploring the use of oral history and life story work with people with learning difficulties in order to enable individuals and groups to tell their stories.

Contact address
> School of Health & Social Welfare
> Open University
> Walton Hall
> Milton Keynes MK7 6AA
> England

Section 4

Advocacy and Empowerment for All

9 Woman to Woman
Setting up and Running a Health Advocacy Group for Women

Doris Clark, Tracey Fry and Jackie Rodgers

Why Did We Want a Women's Group?

The idea for a women's health group came from Kate Eldon and Doris Clark, two women who were active in the local advocacy movement in Bristol. Tracey Fry joined in soon afterwards. Doris and Tracey, who are two of the authors of this chapter, thought of a number of reasons why it was a good idea to have a women's health group:

We thought doctors hadn't explained to us about women's problems and other problems you can get.

We thought women with learning difficulties would talk to us, especially with no men around.

It was a chance for people to have someone who will listen to them.

It was a chance to hear from people who knew about things, like the breast screening woman.

It was good for women to have a chance to talk about problems. Some problems are easier to talk about when there are no men there.

Women can say things which are private and confidential.

Women's meetings make it safe for other women to say things and to learn to express themselves and their feelings.

How the Group Got Started

A few things were needed to start the group up: a room, transport, supporters, money and a planning group. Kate and Doris asked women they knew who had an interest or worked in women's health to help, and some agreed to act as supporters. A planning group was set up, which the authors were all part of, and we asked other women we knew who might be interested if they wanted to join. At first the planning group met in the office of Wellwomen Information, a local voluntary group. Later, when Bristol and District People First (the local self-advocacy group) got their own office, we met there.

Money was needed early on to pay for taxis for women to get to the planning meetings and to hire a room to hold meetings for larger numbers of women. Christine Brookes, from Wellwomen Information, gave her time to help set the group up, and they paid for some early expenses. A local health promotion department agreed to put forward some 'pump priming' money to allow the group to make a start. Then, with the help of a supporter, the group applied to the local health authority for money (a one-off grant) to continue running the group. We did not need too much money. The biggest expense was transport, but that was very important to enable women to take part on a regular basis. Being able to provide transport was an important part of the group's success.

The Planning Group

The size of the planning group changed over time, with between five and seven women, and two or three supporters. The women on the planning group had different levels of experience in doing things like this. Some had lots of experience which was good. This meant they were also very busy and involved in lots of other things, so it was harder for them to find time. Other women were fairly or completely new to doing things like this and needed more support to take part. This worked out well. Women who were new to committees gained more skills and confidence as time went by, and women who had the most experience were not left to do everything.

Usually we met about once a month and planned bigger meetings. We met more often when it was nearly time for a bigger meeting. Up to 50 women were invited to the bigger meetings. They were women who people on the planning group knew might be interested. It did not always seem fair that it was only women who the planning group knew that were invited. This was especially true as no Black women came along. However, we could not invite too many women along, and once everyone had thought of people who might want to come, we had plenty of people to invite. We still keep on thinking about ways of including more women, perhaps by having more groups. Women on the planning group were very keen to make sure that the meetings would be good for all sorts of women. One woman invited women from a long-stay hospital ward. Another woman suggested making sure that there was someone who could sign if anyone was deaf. She also knew some Makaton, so she could communicate with people who used this method.

The planning group decided on dates and times for the bigger meetings. We decided what we would talk about at the bigger meetings and how they would be run. We used suggestions from the women who came to the big meetings when deciding what to talk about and do. There were lots of ideas. They are listed on p.132.

We had to be careful not to try and cover too many ideas in one meeting. It seemed to work best when we covered two or three things at the most. The planning group sent out invitations for the bigger meetings. We got a local service called CONNECT to design the invitations so they would look really nice. CONNECT is an information and resource centre on learning difficulties in Bristol. When they had been designed we could just change a few words and use them again and again (see p.133). We offered to provide supporters if anyone wanted it, but in the end people came on their own or with people they knew.

Our Ideas

- *going to the doctor's*
- *having an internal*
- *periods, how men shouldn't know, how we can know more*
- *chance to talk freely about illness, with no men there*
- *safety - what videos are available*
- *exercise*
- *where you live and what it's like*
- *music*
- *smoking*
- *relaxation*
- *effects of taking the pill*
- *change of life*
- *flower arranging*
- *how your body works*

- *going to family planning*
- *eating*
- *period pains*
- *things that have happened to you, accidents and illness*
- *families*
- *hayfever*
- *independence*
- *music*
- *being careful in the sun*
- *helping other people*
- *sex*
- *grief*
- *medicines*
- *raising money*
- *rug making*

- *having your blood pressure taken*
- *how men treat women like slaves*
- *different sorts of cancer*
- *epileptic fits and what to do - first aid*
- *arthritis*
- *relationships with men*
- *working*
- *education courses*
- *sleep*
- *appearance*
- *hygiene*
- *clothes*
- *women's lives*
- *making cakes*
- *patchwork*

Health Choices for Women are supported by Avon Health, Wellwomen Information, Bristol and District People First and Norah Fry Research Centre

HEALTH CHOICES FOR WOMEN

Drawings by C. Mears, Diane, Doris, J Steer, Tracey Fry, Sarah McGreevy, Poster Design Connect

NEXT MEETING
THURSDAY 28 MARCH 1996
10.30 – 12.30
DUNSTAN CENTRE
PENNYWELL ROAD, EASTON

WE WILL BE TALKING ABOUT RELATIONSHIPS WITH MEN AND SEX

Please send the slip below
to Health Choices for Women
c/o Bristol and District People First
Unit 35, Easton Business Centre
Felix Road, Bristol BS5 OHE
If you are coming to the meeting

- -

I will come to the meeting

Name

_____

Address

_____

_____

Phone

In the planning group we also did some more formal work. We made guidelines for keeping our money safe, such as:

- using a box with a key to keep cash in
- having two signatures on cheques to take money out
- keeping a book to record the money paid in and the money paid out.

We thought about an equal opportunities policy (being fair to everyone) and a constitution (how the group should be run). We got examples from other groups to help us with this. When we thought about how the group should be run, we wanted women who came to the bigger meetings to have the chance to join the planning group. We worked out a way to help people understand what was involved and to help them join in. At one of the bigger meetings the women who were on the planning group sat in a semi-circle and told everyone about what was involved. We put some empty chairs in the semi-circle and asked if anyone else wanted to join. Two women did and came and sat in empty chairs. The other women at the big meeting voted for all these women to be on the planning group, by putting up their hands.

We found that when women came to the planning group, they wanted to talk about personal things, as well as plan the big meetings. This could be difficult if we were trying to plan something which was happening soon and the talk turned to personal issues. However, it was also an important part of what the group did. Women on the planning group could do a good job because of their experiences. We decided to talk about personal things for the first half of the planning meetings and do other work for the second half. The meetings lasted one and a half hours so there was enough time for both. This worked out well. We managed to do plenty of work and still talk about things which were also likely to be important to women who came to the bigger meetings.

The supporters who came along to the planning meetings took a back seat as much as possible, helping when women needed advice or where supporters had experience that they could helpfully share. Supporters also wrote up minutes of meetings, with pictures or symbols to make them more accessible (see p.'s 136 and 137). It was the women with learning difficulties in the planning group who ran it. The supporters did not make the decisions, make phone calls or do anything without checking with, or being asked by, the women on the group. This meant the pace of organising the group could be slow at times but it was in the hands of the women themselves.

Sometimes women on the planning group represented it in other situations. They took part in conferences and lectures. One woman took part in a local women's forum. This was difficult because they kept sending lots of information that was hard to understand. The group asked them to send information in a more accessible form, explaining what this meant, and the organisation concerned said they would try. However, the difficult information kept coming. The group decided that we should phone up and say that we were not going to join in any more. One woman phoned up and explained the situation. She had not done much of that sort of thing before, but she did well. Recently, the organisation has been sending out much shorter and more simple information, so the phone call might have had a good effect.

Women on the planning group felt it was a good experience with only a few drawbacks:

It was good to choose the subjects to talk about.

It was good to get more people involved, to get a signer and use Makaton.

I gave a seminar at a conference, I liked doing that.

I helped with lectures and told them about my life.

We all got on quite well together. We went out for a meal, it would be good to do that again.

It was hard work arranging meetings when you are busy. There was lots of work involved in fund raising.

When I broke two bones, it was harder to get around and to meetings.

Notes about the Womens Group meeting on Monday 17th
October.
Tracey, Doris, Marge, Sheena, Kate, Christine were there.

Tracey showed everyone the computer information about

people to get money from. There are 82!

Marge brought the poster. Christine will get it sent out

to all the women. If she can't, Sheena can help.

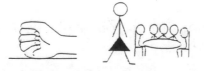

Supporters for Women's Group on 17th November. Sheena
will ask Ruth. Kate will ask Ronda; we agreed to pay
Ronda

Sheena will ask if Jackie spoke to Sally-Ann.

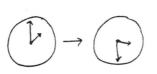

We phoned Diane. Yes, she will be a group leader.

We arranged a training session for group leaders on

Tuesday 8th Nov
2.00-3.30 at People First Office

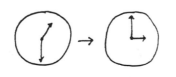

The next planning meeting is Tuesday 1st Nov
                              1.30 - 3.00
                              at People First office

The Big Meetings

The bigger meetings took place three or four times in a year. They usually lasted from 10.30am to 1pm. This suited people who used day centre transport. There was a lot of pleasure and excitement when everyone got together, especially at the first meeting when people saw other women they had not seen for years.

The social aspects of the meetings were very important and plenty of tea breaks were allowed for this. Usually, a woman from the planning group would introduce the day and what we were going to talk about. The planning group made up ground rules for supporters and these were explained to them at the start of the meetings. The planning group and the women who came along to the meetings made up ground rules for them together, to make sure everyone had a fair chance to take part.

Once the ground rules had been agreed, we broke into small groups to discuss whatever the chosen topics were. Someone had the idea of wearing coloured stickers as badges, to help people find their group. Someone from the planning group acted as facilitator for each of the small groups.

Training was provided by one of the supporters for women who had less experience, to help them carry out this role. Their skills and confidence increased over time. The planning group decided that women should be paid a modest amount to act as facilitators. One of the group, or a supporter, recorded what the women wanted to say, using pictures and symbols. These could then be taken back to share with the rest of the women. This was good for women who could not read or write. Jackie's attempts at drawing became a standing joke. She found it hard to draw horses and the women introduced a horse into the conversation at every possible opportunity to get her to draw one! This was typical of the relaxed and friendly atmosphere.

Sometimes a speaker was invited to talk about a topic. A woman from the local breast screening service gave a good talk about breast health. The planning group searched for, or made up, resources relating to the topics chosen, which helped everyone to find out more and join in more easily.

Women from the planning group thought that the big meetings went well:

Arranging the meetings was hard work, but we had prepared in advance, so they ran well.

It was good to ask people what they wanted to talk about.

I was nervous making speeches - I had butterflies in my stomach.

It was good to give people time to speak.

We talked about important things and shared information.

It was good that people got paid to lead the groups.

The Future

It is good that the women's group is not part of any particular service. Women are quite free to say whatever they want, without thinking anyone will get to hear about it, unless they want them to. However, this also meant that the women's group did not have the back up of any organisation, and supporters helped on a voluntary basis, needing a long term commitment. The group is now moving to becoming part of the local People First organisation. This will give it more long term stability, while keeping it in an advocacy environment and without making it part of any service.

It would be good if more women with learning difficulties could go to a women's group. It is helpful for women to have a chance to think about themselves, their bodies and their lives. It is good that women can share private and important matters with people who really understand, and to know they are not alone.

Doris Clark works as a development officer at Circles Network in Bristol. She is chairperson of Bristol and District People First. Doris is on the equal opportunities advisory group of Bristol City Council. She enjoys bingo, the cinema, skittles and TV in her spare time.

Tracey Fry is vice chair of Bristol and District People First. She goes to a day centre. She enjoys doing computer work and drama. Tracey also writes poetry.

Jackie Rodgers is a research fellow at the Norah Fry Research Centre, University of Bristol. Her special interests are health and health care as they relate to people with learning difficulties. She has a particular interest in the health of women with learning difficulties and is currently carrying out research on the experience and management of menstruation.

Contact address
Norah Fry Research Centre
University of Bristol
3 Priory Road
BRISTOL
BS8 1TX
England

10 Self-Advocacy by Black People with Learning Difficulties

Jackie Downer and Peter Ferns

Black Disabled People in Society

In this chapter 'Black' is used as a political term, to stand for solidarity or togetherness for people who experience racism because of their skin colour. By using the term 'Black' it is hoped to give people support and confidence to stand up against racism and not feel alone. It is spelled here with a capital letter to remind us that it is a political term and not just a description of skin colour.

The experience of Black people with learning difficulties is part of the wider experience of Black disabled people in society. Black disabled people have been subjected to a particular form of oppression: a combination of racism and disablism. They are seen in a racist way as aggressive, dangerous, a burden, lazy, less able than they really are, condemned as criminals and more likely to be labelled as schizophrenics. Thinking of groups of Black people in such negative and insulting ways is racist stereotyping and does not give people respect as individuals.

Nor are Black disabled people given chances to have more power over their own lives, to feel confident enough to fight against the discrimination that they face every day. 'Care services' and many of the professionals who work in them are not aware how often Black disabled people have power taken away from them, often by the services themselves. Few services are really suited to the needs of Black disabled people, respect their cultural backgrounds or make them feel strong and confident as Black people.

There are hardly any positive images or role models to give Black disabled people inspiration or a sense of pride. More often they are seen as even more 'pitiful' than white disabled people or more 'tragic' because of poverty in a 'developing' country. Given such discrimination and such attitudes towards Black disabled people, it is not surprising that Black people with learning difficulties are seen as child-like, pathetic and in need of 'care'; or as threatening, aggressive and in need of 'control'.

In this discussion we will put forward some reasons why self-advocacy is particularly important for Black people with learning difficulties, and examine how it can lead to greater 'personal empowerment': that is, having more power and control over your own life. The ideas discussed here come from self-advocacy groups of Black people with learning difficulties in which the authors have been involved.

Common Experiences

The most common experiences for Black people with learning difficulties are:

- having your culture disregarded
- being ignored as a Black person
- being treated as if you were a white person
- being called racist names
- not having your religious beliefs taken seriously
- feeling alone, particularly in hospitals and hostels
- having your confidence taken away
- being given a thousand excuses why you cannot do things
- not being listened to
- being told what to do all the time by staff and families
- having to fight hard to be seen as a strong black person
- having to fight hard for equal respect with others

What is Self-Advocacy?

Self-advocacy can help to reduce negative experiences and increase positive experiences for Black people with learning difficulties. We asked members of Black advocacy groups to tell us what speaking up for themselves meant. They came up with the following answers:

- thinking for yourself
- saying what you think
- having relationships like anyone else
- people listening to you
- making mistakes
- taking risks
- changing people's racist views about yourself
- taking responsibility for yourself
- making decisions
- feeling good about yourself
- feeling good about your own culture and way of life
- standing up for your rights
- getting respect for who you are, as a Black person with learning difficulties.

Why Self-Advocacy?

Making sure people listen to you and know what you want is very important for people who have little power and are likely to be treated unfairly. There are lots of different ways of getting your views and interests across to workers and professionals in care services but speaking for yourself is by far the best. People are likely to be much more confident about their own abilities and have greater control over their own lives if they are enabled to speak for themselves.

Self-advocacy helps all people to know what they really want and be stronger in standing up for their rights. It further helps Black people with learning difficulties to be proud to be Black and disabled, and challenge the negative images in the newspapers and on television. Black people with learning difficulties often need their own space before they feel confident about being on equal terms even with non-disabled Black people.

People in power in care services, usually white people, have to listen to Black service users to provide suitable services in terms of culture, food, dress, ways of life, religions etc. Black people should have respect for their own culture and be helped to deal with racism. One very important source of support for Black service users is their own families. Services should support Black families and help Black communities understand the needs of disabled people.

Black people with learning difficulties must also deal with lack of understanding and prejudices about disability within Black communities and sometimes their own families. This is not to suggest that people might want to leave their families or weaken their ties, but that they may need help in getting their own interests across. Many Black parents and carers themselves need support because of their own experiences of racism in services.

What is a Self-advocacy Group?

A self-advocacy group has to:

- be independent of services and workers;
- have funding without any 'strings' attached;
- be controlled by people with learning difficulties;
- be advised by experienced disabled people and/or non-disabled people skilled in enabling self-advocacy;
- not be shaped by the 'outside' expectations of non-disabled people;
- be given space and time to grow and develop;

- be built on the strengths of the group members;

- be taken seriously by services which should not pretend to support self-advocacy when they really do not;

- have their advice and decisions listened to carefully and acted upon by service workers;

- have real power and representation in important decisions about services which affect users' lives;

- become a pressure group for positive change in services;

- empower group members to change their own lives with the support of other disabled people.

Barriers to Black Self-Advocacy

The main barrier to self-advocacy by Black people with learning difficulties is that other people often do not really want to listen. There is a lot of 'tokenism' or pretending to listen to disabled people, whether they are Black or White, but racial prejudice can result in discrimination even within the self-advocacy movement itself. For example, very few Black people are actively involved and representation in self-advocacy groups is poor. The racist view is that Black disabled people do not have anything positive to say and Black people with learning difficulties are especially likely to be seen as child-like and not very responsible.

Another major barrier is the threat felt by workers and professionals in care services when service users start to make demands and challenge their power and authority. If the group making the challenge is Black, this increases their feelings of being threatened. The lack of Black workers and professionals with real influence makes such challenges less effective since those in power are usually white, non-disabled people. Awareness must be raised generally about self-advocacy and its importance for good quality services, and within Black communities especially.

Difficulties and Benefits in a Black Self-Advocacy Group

We have found that transport and getting around the community are big problems for many group members. Transport is often hard to arrange or arrives late. Sometimes staff from a residential or day care establishment would drive a minibus or car, but only if enough staff were on duty. Often group members who could come to the group on their own were either not allowed to or lacked the confidence. Finding the best time to meet could be difficult if some people preferred to meet during the day and others in the early evening. We held most of our meetings in the evenings, but we have also been involved with daytime groups.

Whatever time is agreed, for people living in residential establishments the attitudes of staff are very important and can decide whether people attend or not. We have practiced dealing with staff who are reluctant to bring people to meetings because they are busy or do not see them as important. We have found that staff feel threatened by the meetings because they do not know what goes on and cannot see any 'results' in their terms. White staff in particular and white service users are also often uneasy about Black people meeting together because it reminds them that racism is still a problem for Black people.

The meetings themselves can be difficult, because group members are not used to speaking out and saying what they feel. People who are used to being told what to do find it hard doing things for themselves and are afraid of making mistakes until they see that this is a way of learning. It takes time for them to overcome these difficulties and feel comfortable in the group.

The benefits are that people become excited and interested, find it easier to talk and become more confident about themselves and their opinions. They feel more important and feel good about being Black, because they have stood up for themselves and made decisions for themselves, and because they have found out more about what other Black people are doing in this country. There has also been a lot of interest in the groups in Black history and the cultures of different countries.

Service Support for Self-Advocacy Groups

To actively support self-advocacy for service users, services and service workers should follow these guidelines:

- Make a public commitment to support self-advocacy and to recognise that it is an important way of empowering users.

- Take positive steps to make sure that self-advocacy happens in residential and day care establishments.

- Inform Black communities about the value of self-advocacy for disabled people.

- Set up systems for talking to self-advocacy groups and take their views seriously.

- Support and encourage Black disabled people to be part of service planning.

- Get resources to support and develop self-advocacy.

- Make sure that self-advocacy is put into practice in all areas of daily living.

- Help people set up self-advocacy groups without taking them over and making them part of services.

- Find Black advisers to self-advocacy groups who are not part of the local services and are as independent as possible.

- Make sure that self-advocates are given real power in decision-making services.

- Give Black disabled people time and space to meet as self-advocates.

- Provide people with the necessary assistance to attend self-advocacy groups, such as transport.

- If a person wishes to attend a self-advocacy group, look on this as very important.

- Train both Black and White staff managers about self-advocacy, and provide training for white users about race issues.

- Train workers to develop skills to help disabled people take more part in every day living tasks, choices and decisions.

- Help Black disabled people to be more involved in training staff.

Postscript

This chapter comes from a workshop given by Jackie and Peter, and published originally in *A Challenge to Change: practical experience of building user-led services*, edited by Peter Beresford and Tessa Harding (London: NISW, 1993).

Although the chapter was written quite a long time ago, it seemed to still have some very important things to say about why self-advocacy matters. Jackie however wanted to make the following comments about what has happened since the chapter first appeared.

> *Things should have improved in self-advocacy for black people with learning difficulties over the last five years. There should be more groups. Instead groups have been cut. There isn't the money for self-advocacy that there should be. Everybody is just surviving and some things have gone backwards instead of forwards. People have to keep pushing for change. If we don't push, nothing happens. I don't want there to be another book in five years time that is still saying the same thing without things actually changing.*

Jackie Downer is a black women with learning difficulties who is a self-advocacy development worker, service user and trainer. She has run many workshops and training events for professionals and black people with learning difficulties with support workers as well as working to establish self-advocacy groups for black service users. She is committed to the development of better community care services for black people.

Peter Ferns is a black training consultant with many years' experience in services for people with learning difficulties. He has wide experience of training and consultancy in public and independent sector organisations on issues of self-advocacy, equality and service development.

Contact address
Peter Ferns
217 New Bedford Road
Luton
Bedfordshire LU3 1LL
England

11 It's Never Too Late
Empowerment for Older People with Learning Difficulties

Jane Fitzgerald

Empowerment for any individual necessitates giving them a voice, listening to what they say, and most importantly, actually hearing it. For older people, many of whom have never had a voice, it is all the more important that we find ways of hearing them.

Historically, people with severe and profound learning difficulties rarely lived to grow old. The older generation of people still living in institutions are often those people who were institutionalised for being 'morally defective'. They have lived in hospital for 40 or 50 years or even longer and they are now facing the prospect of a new life, away from the institution. Many are afraid of moving out. All they know is within the institution; starting again is a daunting prospect. Resettlement for them needs to be handled sensitively and to happen slowly, taking time to enable people to express their apprehensions. It can and does work. Recent research (Fitzgerald, 1998) has shown that people can be effectively resettled regardless of their age. Asking people what they want is an important first step.

Advances in health care mean that people with severe and profound learning difficulties are now living longer; more people who do not use traditional forms of communication need to be 'heard' as to what they want for their future. Providers need to explore different ways of communicating with people to ascertain their wishes.

The people who provide services hold the key to progress in empowerment for older people with learning difficulties. At present, there are few clear plans for the development of services for older people. Ideally each individual should receive a service fitting their needs and wishes, but that rarely happens.

Little thought and few resources are given to providing meaningful daytime occupation and recreation for older people with learning difficulties. So many older people with learning difficulties attend adult training centres which for some may be noisy, distracting and serve no useful purpose. Others do not have anything to do at all during the day. For an older person with a learning difficulty it is like a lottery; being in the right service whose philosophy is centred on listening to what people using the services actually want can mean the difference between living and merely waiting to die.

The following stories of three people interviewed for my research (Fitzgerald, 1998), illustrate the differences which exist in services for older people with learning difficulties and the degree to which they empower them to make choices about the kind of lives they want to lead.

Eve

As a young woman, Eve met and married a soldier. He died during the second world war. Eve had previously lived with her family and, at some point following the death of her husband, she had to move into a local mental handicap hospital. It is not clear why this happened. Eve moved around different hospitals before moving into a large institution in the North West of England. She spent many years there, working hard both on the ward and in the industrial training centre.

In the early eighties, Eve was discharged from the hospital into local housing association accommodation with support provided by a small community service. Eve was not happy here; she did not get on with one of the people with whom she lived and wanted to move out. Her support workers were the key to enabling Eve to find somewhere suitable to live.

At this time, all of Eve's money was controlled by the Court of Protection. She could not access any of her money directly and everything she spent had to be accounted for. This was a major inconvenience in Eve's life and was a priority for her support workers to sort out. Eve received a giro cheque through the post for a set amount; if she wanted to buy anything else, she had to apply to the Court of Protection saying why she wanted extra money. Eve was quite capable of managing her own money but getting out of the control of the Court of Protection was not going to be easy for her. However, her support workers were determined to do what they could to enable her to establish control of her own money. They enlisted the assistance of Eve's GP who was more than willing to write to the Court of Protection to tell them that, in his considered opinion, Eve was quite capable of managing her own affairs. He did this and Eve was finally given control of her own finances.

When Eve and her support worker were discussing where she would like to live, Eve made it clear that she would like to live on her own in her own home. Her support workers listened to what she wanted; between them they decided to look into the possibility of enabling Eve to purchase her own home. As Eve had been resident in housing association property for a number of years, she had become entitled to a discount on purchase of a housing association property. She and her supporters looked around for a suitable property. Eve decided on a ground floor flat which she could manage on her own with minimal support. She purchased the flat. She is helped in managing her finances by an independent financial advisor, and is assisted with any support needs she has by a member of the support team whom she calls 'my staff'.

Eve makes use of a number of community facilities in her home town. She attends classes of interest at the local college; she goes to art classes and attends weekends away with the art group. She holidays abroad at every opportunity and even started to learn Spanish for when she holidays in Spain. Eve plans all of her own time; she does whatever she wants to do. She feels that she has the freedom to come and go as she pleases and does not have to answer to anybody. Her support worker is there when Eve needs her, though Eve has total control over her own decisions.

Eve's life has been enriched through the foresight and creativity of her support team. They not only listened to what she wanted; they truly heard her. Their philosophy is that they are there to support an individual to pursue whatever she or he wants to pursue. As a result, Eve now lives her life as any other person would. She is not constrained by policies and procedures that restrict and cosset people rather than encouraging them to go out and experience life.

The future looks bright for Eve; she has her own home and support workers who encourage and support her in pursuing whatever she chooses to do. However, the support Eve receives is limited to 37.5 hours per week. At present this is adequate and Eve is not restricted in any way. But what happens if the time comes that Eve needs greater support to live her life the way she chooses? Eve is fortunate; she has the financial means to increase the support she receives should she ever need to, but what would the future hold if that were not the case? Would Eve have to move away from her home so that she would have gone full circle from the institution, back to institutional care? Thankfully, that should not happen for Eve, but it may well happen for others. The freedom so longed for through years endured in the institution may be all too brief for some.

Gwen

Gwen has spent most of her life in institutions. There is scant record of her past; there are many lost years where it seems nobody knew or cared where she lived. When the last institution she lived in closed down, she was placed in a large 'unit' where she still lives, as there was nowhere else for her to go. It is not appropriate for her needs. She is in her sixties and the other people living there are in their thirties. The 'unit' is due to close within a couple of years and Gwen will be moving again. This time it is important that she has a say in where she goes and with whom. Gwen is able to speak yet her communication with others is hindered by the defence mechanisms she has set up to protect herself. She has moved around a lot and had many different carers who have come into and then gone out of her life. The only constant thing in Gwen's life has been Gwen. Probably because of her unsettled life and never really belonging anywhere, Gwen has put up a barrier around herself. When she speaks to people she does not know, or if she is in a stressful situation, she tends to repeat certain phrases rather than hold a conversation. It is as though she has decided to protect herself from being hurt by keeping a distance from people and not allowing her emotions to surface through speech.

Gwen was introduced to Paul who works with an organisation which produces multi-media profiles for people with learning difficulties. Paul spent a long time getting to know Gwen, going out with her away from her living environment to experience new and different things. As their relationship developed and Gwen began to trust Paul, they started work on creating a profile of Gwen's life. The profile enables Gwen to tell her story through the use of photographs, pieces of film and sounds which describe the places she has lived, the people who are important to her, what she likes and dislikes and so on. Together they build up a picture of Gwen's life, who she is and what she wants, in such a way as to allow new people who enter into her life a glimpse of who she is.

The profile has given ownership of her life and identity back to Gwen. Previously the only recorded details of Gwen's life had been scant case notes, written by various different people from their own perspective, with little regard to how Gwen may have chosen to record, or not record, those details. Gwen had no say in what was recorded in the notes and no sense of ownership of the contents. They acted to reinforce the institutional way Gwen has always lived, personal details recorded in medical terms, hasty notes written about a particular activity she may have done. There was nothing recorded about what makes her laugh or the music she likes to listen to. Her sense of humour which is so evident in the multi-media profile would have no mention in the brown folder which sat on the shelf in the office.

Case files are not about who an individual is, they are about data, medication, plans, finances and so on. Yet they are all that some people have to show who they are. People who do not use traditional forms of communication and are not easily able to communicate who they are, find themselves defined by text written by numerous people who may or may not know them. The essence of who they are is simply lost in the bureaucracy which governs their lives.

Gwen's multi-media profile does not record meaningless data which means nothing to her. It is not under the control of those who support her. It is entirely hers. Gwen says who does or does not see it and Gwen says what does or does not go into it. The profile is assisting Gwen to tell her story the way she wants it to be told. It is enabling her to finally gain a sense of her own identity. For Gwen, the development of her profile is a very important step in empowering her to define her sense of self and her own future. It has taken over sixty years for Gwen to find her voice and to claim a history of her own.

These two stories illustrate how finding ways of not just listening but truly hearing people and giving them a voice is the all important first step along the road to empowering them to take control of their lives. Age should not be a barrier to empowerment. As Gwen and Eve have shown, it is never too late.

Nobody Listens

However, there are many older people with learning difficulties who do not have a voice. Their lives are controlled by other people. They do not have any say in their own future because nobody wants to listen, yet they have much to say. One such person is Philip.

Philip

Philip lives in an institution which has no plans to close. He is 87 years old and it is expected that he will die where he is and never regain the freedom he and countless others fought for. As a young man he was a soldier in the second world war; he fought for his country, for the freedoms that we all take for granted today. He won three medals for his actions. He was shell shocked in 1942 and returned to England for treatment. In 1943 he was admitted to a psychiatric hospital for further treatment. As the years rolled by, Philip worked at the hospital, making beds and polishing floors amongst other things. His comrades returned from the war, hailed as heroes and began their new lives as civilians. Philip remained in hospital. The hospital changed from providing a service to people with mental health problems into a hospital for people with learning difficulties. Many of the people living there simply stayed on. Philip was one of them.

Philip has a significant amount of money but this does not benefit him in any way. He rarely goes out and is allocated about four pounds a week to spend as he wishes, though he does not like to buy much as it gets stolen by the people he lives with. He does not have his own room; he has a bed in a dormitory which is partitioned off from the others with flimsy walls and curtains. He does not have anywhere to lock things away to keep them safe; his belongings are on open view to anyone who fancies them. The three medals he was awarded for services to his country as a soldier have been either lost within the hospital, or stolen. It is unclear what has happened to them. Nobody cared enough to find out. His honourable past counts for nothing. He recently suffered a hip fracture through being pushed over by one of the younger men with whom he lives.

Philip is not afforded any dignity or respect where he lives. He has ill-fitting dentures which continually fall down, making it difficult for him to speak, which he finds humiliating as he is a very proud man. This has been the case for at least two years, yet nobody cares enough to do anything about it so it goes on.

Philip has been denied any ordinary life opportunities since he was admitted to hospital 55 years ago. The policy of the ward where he lives is that the staff do not discuss resettlement unless one of the people living there asks about moving out. But if the impetus for change has to come from an individual who knows only the limited experience of the institution, nothing will change. Nobody has ever discussed the possibility of moving out with Philip in the entire time he has lived in hospital. He has moved between hospitals and lived in different wards but he has never been given back the freedom which he fought for the rest of us to enjoy.

Where older people have had their entire life dictated by those in authority, either in care situations or protected by family members, and have never been enabled to exercise any control over even the most basic decisions in their lives, empowering them to make decisions and take control of their lives is a long and difficult process. But that should not be a barrier. Increasing age does not have to mean increasing dependency and reducing or suppressing autonomy. The examples of

Gwen and Eve show that age need not be a barrier to discovering a sense of self.

With a positive and creative attitude and a drive to facilitate a person-centred approach to services, things can change. People who have never had the opportunity to make their voice heard and to grow as individuals can be empowered to take control of their own future.

Reference

Fitzgerald, J. (1998) *Time for Freedom?* London: Values Into Action.

Jane Fitzgerald has worked with people with learning difficulties for many years in residential support and with them, their families and carers in the community. She has also studied law and has a keen interest in health care law and medical ethics. She now works freelance in research and training. Jane recently carried out research (funded by the Joseph Rowntree Foundation) for Values Into Action which looked at services for older people with learning difficulties from the perspective of the older people themselves, published as *Time for Freedom?*

Contact address

    Values Into Action
    Oxford House
    Derbyshire Street
    LONDON
    E2 6HG

12 A Say in My Future
Involving People with Profound and Multiple Disabilities in Person Centred Planning

Helen Sanderson

Introduction

Over recent years, advocacy and empowerment have become important issues. Cynics would describe them as the latest buzz words that services use with little understanding, and without applying the concepts behind them. Nevertheless, important advances have been made. People First, an international movement of self-advocacy groups have challenged the way that people with learning difficulties are perceived, described and treated. However, this change in how people are seen is happening very slowly for people labelled as having profound and multiple disabilities. Supporting advocacy and empowerment for people with profound and multiple disabilities requires that we first change our limited expectations and stereotypes:

> *The existence of the most severely mentally handicapped patient is merely vegetative. The patient is mute, completely helpless and lies in his cot showing no awareness of his surroundings, doubly incontinent, and throughout his life requires the same nursing attention as a small baby.*

You would be forgiven for thinking that this must represent the view of people in the 1950s, but Gary Latchford found this description in a textbook on mental handicap published in 1984 (Heaton-Ward and Wiley, 1984, p69). Latchford suggests that this stereotype is only slowly changing and that many people still view people with profound and multiple disabilities as requiring constant care and being unable to comprehend anything around them. In his PhD research, *Towards an understanding of Profound Mental Handicap* (1989), Latchford examined (using video analysis and questionnaires) the characteristics of a group of representative individuals with profound and multiple disabilities. This provided a wealth of information. It demonstrated that people with profound and multiple disabilities are generally aware of their environments and responsive to carers' communication with them; people had a sense of humour; and demonstrated a wide variety of preferences, for example, for Frank Sinatra records or travelling in cars. Most existing definitions and descriptions of people with profound and multiple disabilities focus on what they cannot do, their 'deficiencies'. We need to re-examine and confront these negative stereotypes if the beginnings of self-advocacy for people with profound and multiple disabilities is to advance instead of being treated as a dream.

This chapter begins by identifying what advocacy and empowerment mean in relation to people with profound and multiple disabilities and then looks in detail at how people can become more involved in planning their lives through person centred planning.

Advocacy and Empowerment with People who have Profound and Multiple Disabilities

Self-advocacy for people with profound and multiple disabilities embraces the same underlying principles as any form of self-advocacy. Definitions often include 'speaking up for ourselves' 'self expression' or 'self determination'. With people who have profound and multiple disabilities, who may not use traditional means of communication, supporting self-advocacy means finding ways to understand people and hear what they are communicating, and ensuring that their preferences and desires are acted upon.

As one self advocate explained: 'Self-advocacy is more than speaking up for ourselves, it's actually being what we are too.' (Sutcliffe and Simons, 1993, p.10). It can take many forms, indeed as Skelton (1996) suggests, it is often those actions which the rest of society might not value highly, that can prove to be the most ground breaking examples of self-advocacy. For example:

> *After six months, Dennis has learned to choose his own food*
> *and what to wear. Last week he said 'no' for the first time!*
> (Adult education tutor, cited in Sutcliffe, 1990, p31)

People First of Yeovil extend our definitions of self-advocacy. They compiled a list entitled *How adults with learning difficulties see self-advocacy* (1990). These statements included: 'speaking up for yourself'; 'looking after yourself'; 'being listened to'; 'being with people'; 'friends and friendship'. These are areas of people's lives where person centred planning can be used to try to make them a reality.

In the rest of the chapter we will be focusing on what self-advocacy can mean for people with profound and multiple disabilities in person centred planning. We begin by identifying what person centred planning is.

Person Centred Planning

Person centred planning is the collective term for a family of planning styles which share common principles. Each planning style is used to answer two fundamental questions:

> *Who are you and who are we in your life?*

> *What can we do together to achieve a better life for you now*
> *and in the future?*

This involves a process of learning about a person; who they are; what has happened to them; what is important to them; what they like and dislike; and what they want from life. It means helping people to plan for the future they desire. Person centred planning brings people together to solve problems; build and grasp opportunities; influence communities and change organisations. This takes place over a period of time usually beginning with a planning meeting (Sanderson, Kennedy, Ritchie and Goodwin, 1997).

Person centred planning is *not* the new trendy way of doing individual programme planning with coloured pens and poster paper. Instead it reflects a different way of valuing people, sharing power and being creative rather than fitting people into existing services.

In traditional ways of planning with people, the process often begins with professional assessments where the person is described in terms of what they cannot do - their deficits. This tends to result in setting goals to try and 'fix' these deficits. One of the effects of this is that people are only given opportunities when staff feel they are 'ready'. Traditional planning was used to answer the question 'what can we do to make you more independent?' Person centred planning asks, 'what we can do together to improve the quality of your life?'. Involving people with profound and multiple disabilities in person centred planning requires that we focus on what it takes to involve people in developing the plan, in the planning meeting itself and in implementing and monitoring the plan.

Involving People in Developing the Plan

Involving people in the development of their person centred plan, means that we must find ways of ensuring as far as possible that the plan reflects their preferences. As we are continually learning about the people, sometimes this will reflect our 'best guess' at how the person wants to live their life. Different planning styles present a different lens for looking at the person's life. Some planning styles focus on recording how the person communicates and how they prefer to be supported. Other planning styles include recording the person's history or our understanding of their dreams. It is beyond the scope of this chapter to describe the different styles of person centred planning, and the following is relevant whether Path, Personal Futures Planning, Maps or Essential Lifestyle Planning is used. For descriptions of these planning styles the reader is referred to *People, Plans and Possibilities* (Sanderson, Kennedy, Ritchie and Goodwin, 1997).

Involving people in recording their history

A sense of our own identity - of who we are - is crucial to all of us. It guides us in the decisions we make and the paths we take during our lives. We gain some of that sense through looking at our histories. We have different ways of recording our lives. A consequence of our service system is that a person's label can sometimes become the most important thing about them. Through using a person centred planning process we can learn about the person's history through different people's eyes rather than the perversions of the service system's records.

When beginning to think about how we can support someone to record their story it is worth beginning by looking at our own lives. Many people develop collections of video, photos, certificates, a family tree, stories passed down generations or other ways of recording their life. Supporting people with profound and multiple disabilities in recording their pasts can involve some of the following ideas:

- Going with the person to 'interview' and record on tape people from their past, or who are still in their life, about their memories of the times they spent together. This usually involves asking people about good times that they have enjoyed together, amusing stories or significant events.

- Buying or putting together tapes of the music that the person may have listened to as a teenager.

- Collecting objects with the person, that may represent significant events or people from the past.

- Collecting photographs or pictures of people and events. These could be made into a photo family tree, or album.

- Visiting places where the person has lived, attended school or were significant in some way with the person and taking photographs, video or audio tape. Putting these together with narrative to explain their significance.

Fariana

Fariana is described as having profound, multiple disabilities, challenging behaviour and a visual impairment. Her family came from Pakistan when she was four. Fariana lives in a shared house and her family live a few miles away. Fariana's keyworker, Kate, supported her to develop her life history. It is difficult to know how much Fariana understands, but she talked with Fariana's family about different ways they could tell her story and try to make it as accessible to Fariana as possible. They chose a dowry box, an important part of Fariana's culture, and looked for things to put in it that Fariana could hold that related to her past and what is important to her now. They filled it with many things; for example, a tape of her sister talking about her childhood, a piece of her Mother's sari, some joss sticks similar to those that her family uses. At the beginning of Fariana's person centred planning meeting, Kate and Fariana's sister opened the box and talked about what each item represented. Through this process the team learned more about Fariana and her culture.

Where a person uses objects of reference for communication, as Fariana did, using objects to represent their past as well could be seen as a natural extension of this[1]. The team supporting Fariana initially thought that they would keep Fariana's objects of reference (for example, her cup that she used to take into the kitchen if she wanted a drink) in the same place as the objects that reflected her past. On reflection they decided that this could be more confusing for her and that objects that represented her

---

1   Objects of reference are objects that can be made to signify activities, people, places etc. Ockelford (1994) describes how objects can be used to represent different concept groups such as activities: (e.g. a cup for 'drink', a spoon for 'lunch', a towel for 'swimming'); places (a key for the front door of home); and people (a particular watch or key fob). Objects of reference can be used to develop communication, to help memory and to develop understanding.

present and her past needed to be kept separate. It could be argued that we have no idea whether Fariana's involvement in the process of collecting, or keeping, them made any sense to Fariana. She had interesting trips out and a box of objects which she sometimes sought out and emptied, yet we do not know whether they were meaningful to her in terms of her history in the way that we hoped.

However, even if it was not significant in terms of recording her past for her, it had many effects on the staff team. It made us stop to think about what our understanding was of her communication and what could be relevant to her. It made us research her history and learn things about her that were previously unknown to the service. Our relationship with her family improved as they joined with us to record her past. Our understanding of Fariana, her history and her culture grew. When new staff are now introduced to Fariana, they look through the box with her and an established staff member explains the significance of each object. This must be a better way of involving the person in helping staff to learn about their history than staff reading their 'significant life events' file in the office.

People First in Manchester have made a video of six people who have used different media to record and share their life stories called *My Life, My Story* (People First Manchester, 1997). It includes Fariana's story and those of two other people with profound and multiple disabilities.

Discovering and recording preferences

As well as learning about someone's history with them, we need to learn about their life and preferences today. We need to know about people they associate with, the places they go and the activities that they do. Learning from someone about what their life is like and what they want from it involves spending time with the person and listening to them - to their behaviour as well as their words. John O'Brien describes this as 'listening with your heart'. When the person has profound and multiple disabilities and does not use words to communicate, then discovering the different ways in which they express themselves would be the first step. Learning about the individual may also involve talking to other significant people in their life and spending time with the person. This is a different and more empowering way of learning about the person than just using assessments that describe what the person cannot do.

Spending time together

Many people have been using what is known as the 'Getting to Know You' approach which was originally developed by Brost and Johnson in 1982. This involves discovering who a person is and what their life is like by spending time with them in different places, and talking to people who know them well. It may include looking for relevant information records and case notes. This approach is invaluable if you are assisting someone you do not know well to prepare for their planning meeting or if you are sent to 'assess' someone for a service. More recently, Mark Burton and Carolyn Kagan (1995) have developed these ideas. Spending time together is the cornerstone of learning about what life is like for the person and how they would like it to be. We can learn this even where the person does not use words to communicate.

To learn with someone about what their life is like, we need to be with them during different times and in different places, and with different people doing a range of activities. These may include:

- Sharing an evening meal
- Going to a leisure activity together
- Spending some of a weekend, a weekday morning and an afternoon together
- Spending an evening together
- Being there when there is not much going on
- Attending a meeting with the person or about the person if they do not usually attend
- Trying an activity that is new to the person

Professionals are often very concerned with being objective and detached, but Burton and Kagan encourage us to try and imagine what life is like for the person, to 'get beyond the jargon that often disguises a rather distasteful reality.' Ask 'What would this be like if it was me, or my mum, or my cousin or someone else close to me?' (Burton and Kagan, 1995).

Talking to people who know the person: asking different questions

In getting to know a person who does not use words to communicate, it is essential to find out how they communicate and be aware of many subtleties which are easily missed. It is important to find out who knows the person well and who is able to read the sometimes slight changes which can tell us so much if we know what we are looking for. As well as learning about how the person communicates we need to discover what their preferences are, what is essential for their quality of life, who and what are important to them.

One way to discover this for people who don't use words to communicate (in addition to spending time with them) is talking with other people who know and care about the person. Other people can add valuable insights about what seems important to the person as well as what their past has been like. The individual's family, friends and former support staff can be a source of stories and anecdotes which greatly contribute to seeing the person as an individual rather than their being narrowly defined by assessments.

Getting to know the person in this way requires that we discover the answers to other questions rather than the more familiar 'what does the person need to learn next' approach. We need to think about the different sorts of questions that we can ask whilst spending time with people and supporting them to tell their own story. These questions, based around the Five Accomplishments (O'Brien and Lyle O'Brien, 1991) may be useful:

- Where do they spend their time?

- How can we work together to increase the number of places in the community where they are with other ordinary people ?

- What are the opportunities in the community for the person to pursue their interests and make friends?

- How can we increase these opportunities?

- What contribution can they make to the local community?

- Are there aspects of the person's culture or religion that they may want to explore more?

- What choices does the person make now?

- How can we work together to increase the number and significance of these choices ?

- Who does the person know and spend time with now?

- How can they meet and get to know more people?

- How can their existing relationships be supported?

- Who could help them make changes in their life?

- What does the person enjoy doing? Where do these activities take place? Who do they share these with?

Another different question to ask concerns the person's dreams.

Dreaming

Some styles of person centred planning also involve discovering the individual's dreams. In the context of person centred planning, dreaming is the process of articulating what the person may have always wanted and therefore what is most important to them. Dreaming is one of the most controversial aspects of person centred planning. Where people do not use words to speak, other people who know and care about them, close staff, family, friends are asked to suggest what they think the person's dreams could be. Without a very good knowledge of the person's preferences this could simply represent the group's own dreams, and many people are sceptical about dreaming on this basis.

Pauline
Pauline does not use words to communicate, and the team who support her had spent two years focusing on learning how Pauline communicated and what was important to her through

Essential Lifestyle Planning. They wanted to also think about Pauline's future and decided to use the Path planning framework as a way of doing this. This involved gathering together with Pauline the people who knew her well, and were important to her, to imagine what Pauline's ideal future could look like and then agree actions to take her closer to that.

To achieve this they spent half an hour thinking in pairs about what they had learned was important to Pauline and what she enjoyed, and imagined what life could be like for her, if there were no restrictions on finance or support within a completely inclusive community. They recorded their ideas on 'stickies' and then came together to share their ideas. The group was amazed to see the similarities in what they had put. Each member of the group, from her elderly mother to her key worker, who was the same age as Pauline, suggested a similar dream for Pauline. Pauline is a friendly, outgoing young woman who loves live music and eating out. The dreams all reflected this in the places that Pauline would go to, the people who would support her and that she would live with another woman who shared these interests.

It is possible to dream on behalf of someone and for this just to reflect the dreams and biases of those involved. However, by gathering a range of people who know the person well with an experienced facilitator this is unlikely to happen. Without people who love the person to dream with and find images of a more desirable future, what other ways have we got to suggest direction for the years to come for people with profound and multiple disabilities?

Involving People in Planning Meetings

Asking different questions and finding different ways to understand people helps us begin to answer the first question in person centred planning of 'who are you and who are we in your life?'. The second question 'What can we do together to achieve a better life for you now and in the future?'

is answered when people creatively find ways of making change. This usually involves people meeting together.

Traditionally when we have considered involving people in planning the focus has been on the planning meeting, rather than supporting people to prepare for the meetings and being involved in monitoring actions afterwards. As with traditional planning, there is a danger that people who embrace person centred planning similarly focus on the planning style of the meeting and do not give sufficient attention to the development of the plan or, most importantly the implementation of the plan. Any planning without implementation leaves people feeling frustrated and cynical, which is often worse than no planning at all.

From talking with staff and managers about involving people with profound and multiple disabilities in planning their lives, it seems that people have usually focused on whether the person should be present at their meeting or not. There seem to be three common views on this:

- It can only be tokenistic and therefore people do not bother.

- It is useful for staff to have the person there, regardless of how much the person understands, as it keeps the meeting focused on the person.

- It is the person's right to attend their meeting and therefore staff need to work to make it as accessible as possible.

The first view reflects the stereotype of people with profound and multiple disabilities described in the introduction and a polarised view of people's involvement and contribution. You either involve people fully or else it is completely tokenistic and therefore 'wrong'.

The second view does not seem to address the issue of people's understanding or contribution but instead reflects the perceived benefits for staff of the person's presence: that the tone of the meeting changes when people themselves are there. This may indeed be the case, but the disadvantage of this approach is that the focus is on the staff and how the person's presence may affect them, rather than our responsibility to make the meeting as accessible as possible.

The third view underlines how we need constantly to be working with the person, to be responsive to their communication and to be clear in ours. This should underpin all our time with the person, not just in meetings. The meeting should reflect the ongoing work of learning to listen to the person, to communicate more effectively and evaluate how well we are doing this.

This could be misinterpreted as everyone attending their meeting regardless of any other consideration. We still hear stories of people being locked in the meeting room so that an administrator somewhere could tick the box that states that 'people attended their own planning meeting'. Staff often say attending a meeting would be an unpleasant experience for the person, because they tried it once and it didn't work. Instead of the 'we tried to involve her once' approach, every opportunity should be taken to improve our ability to involve people in a more meaningful way in all aspects of their life.

On many occasions individuals, who were not thought capable of sitting through a meeting, do, because they feel listened to and included and people have seriously thought about what it would take to make it a positive experience for the person.

Steven
Herb Lovett (1996) describes how he used person centred planning with Steven, and how the staff were sure he could not stay in the meeting. Steven was sixteen and described by the staff as having no attention span, could not speak, would become disruptive in the meeting and could not possibly sit throughout it. Herb persuaded them that Steven should start the meeting with them, and that if he needed to leave he could do so, and could rejoin the meeting if he wished. As staff had predicted, at the beginning of the meeting he was noisy and restless and left the meeting with someone for a while. Later he

rejoined the meeting. As part of the planning process that Herb was using, he was asking people what it would have been like to experience what Steven experienced as a child. He described how, as people were talking their tones changed as people considered their own experiences of childhood and reflected on Steven's.

Steven stopped pacing and sat quietly and by the end of the meeting, when people were talking about how he had been systematically rejected by the service and the acceptance that he needed, Steven was curled up calmly, with his head on someone's lap.

'It seemed to me that Steven had done two things. First, he had demonstrated to people how long he could concentrate on things when things were worth attending to. Second, he had served as a barometer for the group. When we began, people were pessimistic and unfocused. They were sure that "he couldn't ... he will never..." By the end ... as the group's optimism and sense of purpose increased, Steven steadily became calmer. Just as he had listened to the heart of people's discussion, they were beginning to learn they could listen to the hidden heart of his behaviour'.
(Lovett, 1996)

This example demonstrates how just changing the tone and focus of meetings can have a significant effect on people, and whether they want to stay there or not. If all that people have experienced are dull meetings, where others have read reports about what they cannot do and where the individuals concerned have had little or no understanding of the content of those reports, then they will not have felt their presence was welcomed.

How much people can understand is one of the issues that most staff bring up when looking at the issue of involving people. Some people think that we should always assume that the person understands what is being said to them and therefore should be included in conversations and meetings like everyone else. People sharing this view will support the person to attend the meeting and will direct conversations towards the person to include them.

Others believe that each of us experience limits to our ability to communicate and that involving people in their planning meeting requires that we understand any differences or limitations in people's communication and respond to that.

We need to work to discover each individual's abilities, or make an informed 'best guess' at this, and use this information to redesign meetings to make them as accessible as possible for people. Including people in conversations is part of this, but each individual will require different ways for us to continually learn how best to include them.

The Views of People First

When writing their booklet *Our Plan for Planning*, (1996), People First in Liverpool and Manchester described their experiences of planning and what they would like to change. Traditional assessments and planning meetings are usually held in an office, with several professionals, sometimes including a parent and occasionally including the individual concerned. The meeting is chaired by one of the professionals: it always takes place during the working day and lasts a set time. Minutes are taken to be typed up and distributed later. People First outline some of the changes they would like to see and for each of these we consider what this could mean in practice for people with profound and multiple disabilities.

'People are given time and support to prepare'

We want to think about what we want for the future and get together ourselves before we involve other people.
(Liverpool & Manchester People First, 1996)

For people with profound and multiple disabilities this means being supported to record their own history, what life is like now and perhaps also what their dreams could be (as discussed earlier). Finding ways to communicate this in ways that are as accessible as possible to the person themselves is one of the biggest challenges in empowering people. Often, the person himself gives us clues about how to do that. For example, Robert used to spend some time each day watching a video of his family. When the staff team who support him started to think about better ways of keeping Robert at the centre of the planning process, they thought about Robert sharing his history and what is important to him now through video. Working closely with his parents they identified significant people and places in Robert's history and went with Robert to video the places. Photographs of key people were also put on to video with narrative to explain who they were. The final part of the video gave people a good understanding of a week in Robert's life by showing him engaged in the typical activities that he is involved in. The video was shown at the beginning of Robert's meeting to help people get a better understanding of what Robert's past and current life was like. Robert sat mesmerised in front of the TV and applauded when it had finished. He still watches the video regularly and the team plan to update it with the new activities that Robert is now involved in as a result of his meeting.

'They are able to choose who attends, the venue and time of their meeting'

> *Not with the managers and staff sitting behind the desk. You should choose nice room, comfy chairs.*
> (Liverpool & Manchester People First, 1996)

For people with profound and multiple disabilities this means thinking about where the person seems most comfortable and at what part of the day they are most alert. For example, some of us are morning people who are most at ease in our own homes. Finding out this information about the individual is important when planning their meeting, so that we can arrange it at the best time and at the most appropriate venue for them. Choosing who to attend also means that we think about who is important to the person from their perspective and not just which professionals are involved in their life. The number of people invited will also need to reflect how many people we think the person would be comfortable to have around.

Jean

The team who supported Jean thought about these issues when they were planning her meeting. Jean attended the local Catholic Church and sometimes attended social events in the hall attached to the Church. She is also a food connoisseur. The team decided to see if they could have the meeting in the Church hall and have a buffet in the middle of the meeting with many of the different foods that Jean enjoys. When thinking about who to invite they drew up a relationship circle which helped them to think about who was closest to Jean. They thought about the Father at the Church she attended, two of the staff who used to support her and who are still in touch, and her Aunt, as well as some of the team members. As Jean is a gregarious and friendly person, they thought that she would enjoy having this number of people around. The meeting seemed very successful and afterwards the team evaluated the decisions they had made on Jean's behalf and whether next time they would try anything differently.

'They are not the objects of discussion but have an active, central role'

You could say what you wanted but it wouldn't happen - it was the ideas staff had themselves that they did.
(Liverpool & Manchester People First, 1996)

For people with profound and multiple disabilities this means trying to find the most accessible ways of communicating information in the meeting. As we have said earlier, this should be an extension of how we listen to the person and communicate with them in every situation rather than something that is peculiar to planning meetings. If the person uses objects of reference then we need to think about whether there are ways of incorporating these into the meeting; if the person uses photos and pictures then we need to think about these.

David

*A pictorial or graphic record has a vibrancy lacking in a list of words and thus has more appeal. People who may be bored during the meeting are often re-engaged through using graphics. This seemed to be the case in David's meeting. David sat through his meeting patiently but it was obvious that his attention was elsewhere. He wandered backwards and forwards. At one point he approached the graphic and his attention was engaged obviously for the first time. He looked at the images which made up other people's dreams for him and when there was talk of his room being painted he indicated that he wanted it painted yellow by choosing one of the pens held out to him. (*Sanderson et al, 1997)

'Emphasis is placed on what people are able to do and what community and service supports are needed to help them achieve their needs and wishes, not repeatedly focusing on what people cannot do'

Plans are not worth bothering about if the same old stuff keeps coming up - it should be good ideas instead.
(Liverpool & Manchester People First, 1996)

For people with profound and multiple disabilities this means focusing on the different questions suggested earlier and using a person centred planning style of meeting rather than a traditional approach that focuses on 'fixing' the person. The final change that People First wanted was to make sure that something happened as a result of the plans.

The person should be involved in the development of the programme and checking how things are going.
(Liverpool & Manchester People First, 1996)

Involvement in Monitoring the Plan

Janice

A positive empowering approach to monitoring plans is being piloted by Manchester Joint Service for a young woman with profound and multiple disabilities called Janice Pearson (Social Services Inspectorate, 1996). Through a person centred planning approach, the team who support Janice identified key features of her lifestyle that were important to her, namely health care, accommodation, personal support, advocacy, communication and leisure activities. These were developed into a contract between the Joint Service and Janice; based on the principle that someone who pays for a service should be able to exercise some control over the service. Reimbursement for failing to meet aspects of the contract is set as a percentage of the charge made to Janice. (The charge for Janice's service is based on the rate of attendance allowance of the care element of the Disabled Living Allowance.) The contract is monitored internally by a member of the Joint Service and by someone external to the service.

Extract from Janice's service support contract

Janice Pearson has the right to expect value for money from the service she is paying for. Where that service falls short of agreed levels or fails to meet its agreed goals she will assert her right to some financial recompense. Failure to meet this target over more than a three week period will result in a reimbursement of £10 for each week the goals are not met.

Janice enjoys movement/crowds and noise especially. Janice must have access to leisure activities at least once a week that accommodate this preference. These activities must include:

- *watching either Manchester United or Manchester City*
- *watching local teams playing where the above is not possible*
- *watching live ice hockey/basketball matches*
- *seeing live bands at a range of venues (including the Apollo, Band on the Wall)*
- *going to dances/discos.*

Developing ways of achieving real accountability to people, based on understanding them through a person centred planning process is one of the challenges of the future. Direct payments (see chapter 15) could be part of the answer, but the key to making this empowering for the individual lies in developing a rich and real understanding of the person. Janice's contract would be meaningless if solely developed by a staff team with an eye on what was possible within current resources rather then investing in really discovering what was important to Janice. Here independent facilitation could play an important role in safeguarding such a process from becoming another bureaucratic exercise.

Conclusion

Involving and empowering people with profound and multiple disabilities in person centred planning needs to be seen as an extension of our commitment to learning to communicate effectively with people and responding to their communication with us. This means asking different questions and learning about people in different ways, to find people's preferences and even dreams. Our approach needs to be one of continually asking what it would take to involve people more in every aspect of their life, and not just planning. Without this perspective, an investment in finding ways to involve people in a planning process that is then, perhaps like the plan itself, filed and redundant until the same time next year is futile. This will just add to our list of service abuses of people with profound and multiple disabilities. Discovering ways of empowering and involving people in developing a plan, in the meeting to agree actions and in implementing and monitoring the plan, is one step closer to self-advocacy for people with profound and multiple disabilities.

References

Brost, M. and Johnson, T. (1982) *Getting to know you.* Wisconsin: Wisconsin Coalition for Advocacy.

Burton, M. and Kagan, C. (1995) *Social Skills for People with Learning Disabilities - A social capability approach.* London: Chapman and Hall.

Heaton-Ward, A. and Wiley, Y. (1984) *Mental Handicap (formerly Mental Subnormality) Fifth edition*. Bristol: Wright.

Latchford, G. (1989) *Towards an Understanding of Profound Mental Handicap.* Edinburgh: University of Edinburgh. (Unpublished Ph.D thesis).

Liverpool and Manchester People First (1996) *Our Plan for Planning.* Manchester: People First, Fourways House, 57 Hilton Street, Manchester M1 2EJ.

Lovett, H. (1996) *Learning to Listen*. London: Jessica Kingsley Publishers.

O'Brien, J. and Lyle O'Brien, C. (1991) *Framework for Accomplishments*. Georgia: Responsive Systems Associates.

Ockelford, A. (1994) *Objects of reference.* London: Royal National Institute for the Blind.

People First Manchester (1996) *My Life My Story*. Manchester: People First, Fourways House, 57 Hilton Street, Manchester M1 2EJ.

People First Yeovil (1990) How adults with learning difficulties see self-advocacy. Quoted in Sutcliffe, J. and Simons, K. (1993; pp 2-3) (see below).

Sanderson, H., Kennedy, J., Ritchie, P. and Goodwin, G. (1997) *People, plans & possibilities - exploring person-centred planning*. Edinburgh: Scottish Human Services.

Skelton, J. (1996) *Exploring issues surrounding self-advocacy for people with learning difficulties, via participant observation.* Manchester: Manchester Metropolitan University. (Unpublished M.Sc thesis.)

Social Services Inspectorate (1996) *Planning for Life - Developing community services for people with complex multiple disabilities. No.2: Good practice in Manchester.* London: Department of Health.

Sutcliffe, J. (1990) *Adults with Learning Difficulties. Education for choice and empowerment.* Buckingham: Open University Press.

Sutcliffe, J. and Simons, K. (1993) *Self-advocacy and Adults with learning Difficulties. Contexts and Debates*. Leicester: NIACE.

Helen Sanderson works as a Quality and Service Development Officer in Manchester. She was seconded part-time to the Joseph Rowntree Foundation funded project on person centred planning, *People, Plans and Possibilities* from 1995 - 1997. Helen has a background in occupational therapy, a Master's in quality assurance in health and social care and is completing her PhD in person centred planning with people with profound and multiple disabilities. She is an Essential Lifestyle Planning mentor trainer and works as a consultant for the National Development Team and Scottish Human Services. She has contributed to course materials for the Open University, Birmingham University, and Manchester University.

Contact address
    34 Broomfield Road
    Heaton Moor
    Stockport SK4 4ND
    England

13 Letting it Take Time
'Rights' Work with Disabled Children and Young People

Ruth Marchant

Introduction

Don't you realise you will raise children's expectations?
(Care Manager of Adult Services)

This paper describes 'rights' work developed with multiply disabled children and young people at Chailey Heritage. The work with young people around rights, advocacy and empowerment has evolved over the last eight years as part of a much wider attempt to take a strong children's rights/child protection agenda into the centre of a large and well established institution.

This paper describes the development of a number of approaches, including a children's charter, good practice guidelines, a young people's group and independent advocacy. Most of these developments affect the whole service and all have involved young people in different ways. We have learnt a great deal in the last eight years, some of it through struggling and some of it through making mistakes. The work at Chailey is by no means 'finished' and we are still unsure about many issues.

The Context

Chailey Heritage is a specialist centre in Sussex for children with complex physical and multiple disabilities, offering education, residential care, medical treatment and rehabilitation. It is a large service with around 100 children attending on an average day, and more than 400 staff and volunteers. The Chailey Heritage site comprises Chailey Heritage School (a non-maintained residential special school for children with complex physical and learning difficulties) and services provided by South Downs Health NHS Trust. These complement the work of the school as well as providing a range of services for outpatients.

Chailey Heritage is involved in different ways with many disabled children and young people. At Chailey Heritage we had been concerned for some years about the links between abuse and disability. We became aware that the young people we worked with faced an increased risk of abuse and wanted to try to make a difference by changing our practice. We felt that some of what we did perhaps contributed to the vulnerable position that children found themselves in, and we felt that maybe we could create an environment where children could be safer and feel more able to tell about abuse.

The Young People

Chailey Heritage has provided for disabled children since 1903, and over time the nature of the children's impairments has changed again and again. Overall the direction of the change has been one of increasing complexity, such that today most young people who come to Chailey Heritage have severe and complex physical disabilities with additional sensory impairments or learning disabilities. Most are reliant on powered mobility and the majority use communication methods other than speech.

Naive Beginnings

Until the late 1980s we believed, like many others, that disability would somehow protect children from abuse. For us the shock of realising that this is not the case led us to think differently about our practice at Chailey, and to try and make some changes.

Some of our early work now seems embarrassingly naive. For example, we looked around for resources to work with children on personal safety and self esteem, and were surprised to find that all of them were written for non-disabled children. Even the pictures were all of non-disabled children. The safety messages were based on skills and resources that weren't available to many of the young people we worked with: messages like 'say no' or 'run away' were devastatingly unhelpful for young people who don't walk or talk; and messages about adults not touching the private parts of your body were frankly confusing for young people who need help with intimate care.

We adapted some existing material and also developed some of our own, and started trying to 'teach' safety and assertiveness skills to groups of young people. This proved extremely difficult. For example, as part of a 10 week programme of sessions a 13 year old girl, Karen, was 'practising' saying no under pressure. She and another young person were role-playing shopping for pop music, and the aim was for Karen to practise refusing the offer of an unwanted alternative. The idea of the exercise was that Karen only wanted to buy a Pet Shop Boys cassette, nothing else. In the role-plays she seemed to find it almost impossible to resist persuasion, for example:

> *Karen (customer) : Have you got the Pet Shop Boys?*
> *Child 2 (shopkeeper): No, sorry, would you like Duran Duran*
> *instead?*
> *Karen: OK, thank you.*

Intellectually Karen was easily able to comprehend the principles of assertiveness and she also had the verbal skills to negotiate. We tried again:

> *Karen: Have you got the Pet Shop Boys?*
> *Shopkeeper: No, sorry, but I've got Duran Duran.*
> *Karen: Are you sure you haven't got the Pet Shop Boys?*
> *Shopkeeper: No. Do you want Duran Duran?*
> *Karen: OK.*

All the young people in the group were very engaged with the role-play, so we went through the idea of refusing again, reminding Karen: 'You don't want to buy anything else. Just the Pet shop boys. You *hate* Duran Duran.'

> *Karen: Have you got the Pet shop boys?*
> *Shopkeeper: No, sorry, but I've got Duran Duran.*
> *Karen: Are you sure you haven't got the Pet Shop Boys?*
> *Shopkeeper: No. Do you want Duran Duran?*
> *Karen: But I don't like Duran Duran.*
> *Shopkeeper: They're very good.*
> *Karen: Oh, OK.*

Karen appeared totally unable to say no to something she didn't want, even in a 'safe' role-play situation.

Then we stopped and thought about Karen's life. She had lived in residential institutions of some kind or other since the age of two. She moved frequently between a residential school and a residential respite unit and there had been a number of concerns about abuse in the little time she did spend at home. There were few areas of Karen's life where she had any real choice or control.

In retrospect we had been incredibly naive to think that Karen might be able to 'learn' assertiveness skills and then make use of them in her life, unless she was able to experience some control over what happened to her.

From this early work we learned that there is no point trying to teach children that they have rights when their experience tells them otherwise. In fact, we came to feel that it could do positive harm to give children such confusing messages that were incompatible with their day to day lives.

The Children's Charter

We realised that if we were serious about rights for disabled children we needed to think about what we *did* as well as what we *said*. We realised that we couldn't change everything but we felt we could try and make a difference to the lives of young people in their time at Chailey, so in 1990 we developed the children's charter at Chailey: a statement of children's basic rights. The charter is designed to give us a bottom line about the way children are treated at Chailey.

We involved young people and also a group of parents in helping us decide what should be in the charter. We were initially surprised that the young people wanted to include some things that we felt were relatively 'small' or unimportant issues, for example about the way they were spoken to or about choosing what to eat or drink. However, over the years we have realised that little things matter enormously to children and young people, and although they can often be a symbol of something bigger, specifying the detail helps everyone be clear about what is expected.

The charter sets out four basic rights for children at Chailey, relevant for every child at all times and thus for everyone involved with the children:

> ## Four basic rights
>
> 1. *to be valued as an individual*
>
> 2. *to be treated with dignity and respect*
>
> 3. *to be cared for as a child first*
>
> 4. *to be safe*

The charter also sets out what these rights mean in practice; for example that treating children with dignity and respect means talking to and about children by their own name, telling children about procedures before they occur etc.

Introducing the Children's Charter

We felt that our practice in terms of rights, choice and control needed to be consistent - not just at certain times of the day, and not just with certain members of staff. Participation in teaching about the charter is therefore compulsory for all staff groups.

The charter is introduced to staff through a presentation that tries to bring to life the ideas about created vulnerability, and to relate these ideas to people's day to day practice and to children's day to day experiences. The presentation involves visual imagery and the acting out of practical examples, and is designed to challenge ways of working and attitudes that can devalue or disempower children. We use examples of things that get said to and about the children we work with, such as this list of real questions asked and comments made over the heads of real children:

> *Is he a Downs Syndrome? Is she spastic? Does she talk? Is he yours? Does she live at Chailey? Will he get better? Was she born like that? Does he always do that? Can't you keep her still? Is he dangerous? Is there a cure for it? Have you claimed compensation? Will he die young? What a <u>shame!</u> Such a pity! It's so sad! His poor parents! Such a tragedy! Poor little thing! He should never have been born.*

We talk about the long term impact of hearing these kinds of things said day after day. The charter presentation teaches that we live in a culture that makes disabled children very vulnerable, by placing a low value on disabled children and often excluding them from the mainstream of life - including from services that protect children. The presentation teaches that it is often not very safe to be a disabled child and therefore the ways we treat children and the messages we give to them and to the outside world about what they are worth really matter.

Struggles with introducing the charter

Most people working at Chailey welcomed the introduction of the charter, although some were concerned about the idea of rights for young people and felt the charter placed them in a difficult position. As the young people at Chailey got to know about the charter some of the more able young people became very articulate about their rights. Sometimes this was in a genuinely informed way; at other times young people have insisted that the charter gives them rights such as to stay up all night; to swear at staff;

to hurt others etc. This has needed careful handling to ensure both that young people gain a helpful understanding of their responsibilities as well as their rights, and to ensure that staff feel confident in responding to young people who can be challenging.

This led us to develop a number of things, including further guidelines about good practice, for example, when handling difficult or challenging behaviour or when seeking a young person's consent to treatment and examination. We also offer direct access for anyone who needs it to a multidisciplinary group - the child protection working group - who can provide support and guidance to both young people and staff. One of the basic beliefs underlying all of this work is that both children and staff are safer if expectations within the service are clear.

Introducing the charter of rights to the young people has not been easy. The range of age, ability and communication skills among those served by Chailey is enormous. Initially we tried various versions of the charter presentation, involving acting out of 'bad' practice, with young people. We ran into difficulties: some young people found role play very difficult to relate to; others seemed to make sense of the 'acting', and clearly recognised the examples acted out but showed no apparent concern. For example, a group of disabled teenagers reacted to the presentation by saying that: 'Yes these things happen to me, most of them everyday.' 'People talk about me as if I'm not there.' 'People stare at me in the street and ask questions.' 'People make decisions without consulting with me.' Many young people were insistent that these things happened to them everywhere: at home, at school, in residential care etc., and that this was just the way it was - the way it always had been and always would be.

Almost by mistake, we introduced the charter presentation to a group of disabled and non-disabled young people together at an integrated youth club at Chailey. This provoked extremely strong reactions from the non-disabled young people, who reacted with incredulity and anger to the presentation: 'Do people really treat you like that?' 'No-one would speak to me that way.' 'How can you let them undress you in front of a whole group of people?' This engendered some very helpful and lively discussions. This work took place over a period of several months as part of an established and supported group.

We have involved disabled adults active within the disability movement in our work. Some of the side effects of this were unintentional but very useful. For example, we discovered that some young people believed that their disabilities would somehow disappear as they reached adulthood, which is not such a silly assumption if most of the children one meets are disabled and all of the adults are not. Just meeting and spending time with disabled adults can have a value in itself. Some of the most constructive resources we have used have been developed by groups of disabled children working with disabled adults (GMCDP, 1996).

Chailey Young People's Group

The Chailey Young People's Group (CYPG) originated with a group of four young people. They met weekly for nine months in 1994, at the request of the Child Protection Working Group, with an independent facilitator. They worked out a detailed proposal for a young people's group, summarised in this letter:

> *We are four young people who enjoy meeting weekly to discuss our feelings about Rights and Responsibilities and how young people are treated at Chailey. We were asked by the Child Protection Working Group to think about ways for young people who come to Chailey Heritage to be able to complain, express their worries or to communicate their opinions.*
>
> *We feel a good way to start is to form a 'Chailey Young People's Group' (CYPG) who will be able to listen if you have a problem, help if you need to complain and put you in touch with someone who can advise you on what to do. When necessary we will find someone who can help us to communicate and we can pass on ideas and concerns to Chailey Heritage on your behalf. This term we shall be inviting others to join us in setting up this first Chailey Young People's Group. We plan to get the help of an 'advocate'*

who will be independent of Chailey Heritage, to help us all by being able to listen and make it possible to be heard. A leaflet will be sent to everyone and posters will be put up around Chailey, explaining how to contact the group when we are able to start....
Thank you for listening to us,
Yours sincerely,
the Student Rights Group

To ensure genuine independence of the advocate we went to an outside organisation for assistance. Chailey Heritage funds the advocacy scheme but the Children's Society manages the scheme and employs the advocate. The young people were involved in vetting the member of staff that the Children's Society recommended to take on the advocacy role. These were some of the questions the young people asked:

Are you a determined person?

Can you be persistent?

Will you be loyal to the young people?

Are you a good listener?

Are you patient?

Will you treat the children and young people as equals? Does that present a problem for you?

Are you willing to give physical and emotional comfort to the young people if necessary?

The process of leaflet and poster design, and the planning of the public 'launch' of the group took 3 months. The cover of the leaflet is shown on p.192 and the content is reproduced on p.193.

In April 1995 the CYPG officially began. The group has fluctuated in size and the membership changes with time. There have been struggles within the group, for example about gender: there was an attempt early on to make the group for girls only. Another early issue was about age: some members felt that you could not be considered a young person until the age of 11. Eventually the group agreed there should be no lower age limit, but in practice the group has had only one member under 11.

For most of the group's lifetime (including the original Student Rights group) the majority of members have communicated other than by speaking. This has meant a need for several facilitators/communicators to be present at each group (usually at least four). These people need to be competent with the communication systems in use by the young people and also able to genuinely listen and put forward others' viewpoints.

Providing support for communication in a setting like the CYPG demands different skills from day to day work with disabled children. For a time we tried volunteer workers alongside the paid advocate but have returned to the use of paid staff. However, the young people have a genuine choice about which adults are present in the group and there are clear expectations on the adults built into the rules of the group.

Listening well to others is one of the aspects of the CYPG most highly valued by the young people. As observed by one member with a speech impairment:

The fact is that you can talk until you are blue in the face but if you have no one to listen it's not going to do you much good.

Chailey Young People's Group (CYPG) enables every young person to meet together and speak out.

It is run by Chailey young people, for all who use Chailey services.

We provide a safe place to have fun and communicate with each other, share points of view, express ideas and help solve problems.

You can attend regularly, or just come along when you have a problem or a view you want to share.

The Chailey Young People's Advocate, who is independent of the organisations providing the services at Chailey, will be at the meetings to help and pass on your ideas and concerns on your behalf.

Here are examples of situations where CYPG could help:

Mary has a problem. A boy in a big wheelchair is teasing her and has run into her. She is too frightened to tell her teacher or her key worker or anyone else about it.

Q. What can she do?
A. Talk to her friends at the CYPG.

John has an idea. He's not sure if it's a good one or if it will work. He would like to know what others think of his idea, but doesn't know who to discuss it with.

Q. What can he do?
A. Talk to his friends at the CYPG.

The rules drawn up by the original Student Rights group were revised and extended by the CYPG after a year:

1. The group is a safe place to talk where things won't be talked about outside, either by group members or staff.

2. The group is a place to bring problems where someone will help you.

3. No-one will laugh at your problems.

4. Young people should be able to speak for themselves unless they want someone to speak for them.

5. Members of the group should be able to communicate with everyone.

6. Members should be able to bring a helper with them to the group.

7. If a member of the group is not happy with the adults they can ask them to leave.

8. When decisions are made, everybody has their say.

9. Members of the group should listen when someone is trying to talk to the group.

10. Group members should have transport to the group every week.

After the first year of the CYPG, the advocacy scheme was extended to allow time for individual advocacy work and for a daytime open access session. Although the independence of the advocate is crucial to the success of the group, support for both the group and the advocate is needed from within Chailey. This involves ensuring awareness of the CYPG and advocacy scheme at all levels: implicit support from the organisation in 'hosting' and funding the scheme; direct practical support for young people wishing to access the advocate or attend the group; behind the scenes work to maintain understanding and support for the group and a willingness at senior level to take seriously any concerns raised by young people.

Lessons Learnt

We have learnt a great deal over the last eight years. The work described above has not always been easy and we have learnt much from our mistakes. Some of the major lessons have been:

- The need for a whole service approach and the need for the service as a whole to accept a shared responsibility for child protection. At Chailey we have been able to involve people from different professional backgrounds: the Child Protection Working Group includes nursing, medical, teaching, child care, social work, therapy and management representation. This has been essential in developing work that genuinely crosses over professional boundaries within the service.

- The value of external involvement from outside the organisation: independent advocacy is central to the functioning of the Chailey Young People's Group. In addition, we have been able to build good working links with the local child protection unit, involving joint working with individual children in investigating abuse (see Marchant and Page 1993, 1997), and also an advisory input from one of the child protection team to the child protection working group at Chailey .

- The 'interconnectedness' of all of this work: the preventative, investigative and therapeutic work are heavily interdependent. Introducing the charter of rights led to a significant increase in the number of child protection concerns, we think by raising awareness that children might be at risk. We do not think more children were being abused; we think we became better at noticing and acting on our concerns.

- The need to change our practice and children's day to day experience. Telling children that they have rights, if their day to day experience tells them otherwise, can be at best confusing, and, at worst, harmful. If what happens to you everyday is that people talk about you as if you aren't there, and undress you without your consent, and give you messages that you should be other than you are and in fact maybe shouldn't be alive at all; if you sleep in four different beds every week and have more than twenty adults involved in your care then it is unlikely to be helpful to be told that you have rights and you have power.

Conclusions

We have been trying to achieve a number of things through the work described above. We wanted to make Chailey Heritage a safer place for children to be. We wanted to encourage a generation of confident, assertive disabled young people; young people who are clear about their own identity; who understand their rights and responsibilities; who have helpful information about relationships and about sex; who are aware of their own needs and those of others.

It hasn't been easy, and along the way questions have been raised by other professionals about what we're doing:

If you teach her that she can have the toilet door closed when she uses the toilet, then she's always going to want the toilet door closed.

If you let him drive a powered chair with chin switches then he's not going to like using a manual chair in future.

If you teach children what their rights are then they're going to be much harder to look after...Don't you realise you will raise children's expectations?

We think that children's expectations need raising. We hope that if children are treated as individuals, and with dignity and respect, then maybe they will be less vulnerable to abuse, and maybe they will be more able to tell if bad things happen to them. And maybe we will be more able to hear if they do tell us.

Acknowledgements

The CYPG leaflet was written and designed by the CYPG with help from Tony Ashton. Illustration by Holly Williams. The Chailey Young People's Advocate is Sue Virgo.

References

GMCDP (1996) *Disability Is...* (video and resource sheets). Manchester: Greater Manchester Coalition of Disabled People (Tel: 0161 273 5154).

Marchant, R. and Page, M. (1993) *Bridging the Gap: Child Protection Work with Multiply Disabled Children.* London: NSPCC.

Marchant, R. and Page, M. (1997) The memorandum and disabled children. In Westcott, H. and Jones, J. (eds.) *Perspectives on the Memorandum: Policy, Practice and Research in Investigative Interviewing.* London: Arena.

Virgo, S. (1998) Group advocacy in a residential setting. In Robinson, C. and Stalker, K. (eds) *Growing Up with a Disability. London:* Jessica Kingsley.

Westcott, H. and Cross, M. (1996) *This Far and No Further: Towards ending the abuse of disabled children.* Birmingham: Venture Press.

Note

A copy of the charter of rights is available free on request from Chailey; please send a stamped addressed envelope. The full set of internal guidelines relating to child protection is available for £5.00 inc. postage and packing. This includes the full version of the charter of rights, and also guidelines for:

- handling concerns about possible abuse
- good practice in intimate care
- working with children of the opposite sex
- handling difficult behaviour
- consent to examination and treatment
- working with children on sexuality and personal development

For more information or to request guidelines contact the NHS Manager, Chailey Heritage (South Downs Health), North Chailey, Sussex, BN8 4JN.

Ruth Marchant works in services for disabled children and also on a training and consultancy basis. She has particular interests in child protection, challenging behaviour and in the emotional needs of disabled children. She works part-time for two Sussex based organisations serving children with complex needs. She co-directs Triangle, which links specialist training and consultancy with direct services for children with severely challenging behaviour, and also works one day a week as specialist adviser at Chailey Heritage, a centre for multiply disabled children and young people.

Contact address
> Triangle, Unit 310
> 91 Western Road
> Brighton
> East Sussex   BN1 2NW
> England

Section 5
Changing Policies and Practices

14 Who Chooses?
Involving People with Learning Difficulties in Staff Selection and Recruitment

Margaret Macadam and Ruth Townsley

If you are going to be working with a certain person you have got to get to know them. You have got to get on with them. So you have to imagine them working with you.
(Day service user)

I have to say that it has been a very positive experience. Clients have been very insightful. I think it's worth saying that we haven't yet had an appointment that hasn't worked out.
(Manager, local authority day service)

The idea of user involvement in community care services has been around for some time now. The principle applies just as much to people with learning difficulties as it does to any other group of service users, yet service providers in this field may still be searching for ways of putting the theory of user involvement into practice. One way forward is to involve people with learning difficulties in staff recruitment.

People with learning difficulties themselves have highlighted this issue as crucial if they are to be fully empowered as partners in planning and delivering services. Indeed it was the work of people with learning difficulties in the Bristol area that prompted us to examine the issue of their involvement in staff recruitment. Representatives from local services had written to the Social Services Committee expressing their concerns about their lack of involvement in recruiting staff. One Bristol self-advocacy group had also conducted a small survey addressing this issue and had found little if any involvement of people with learning difficulties in the recruitment process.

Yet there are clear reasons why this situation should change. Involvement in staff recruitment exemplifies a commitment to promoting choice and control for people with learning difficulties over their daily lives: principles which are central to the concept of self advocacy. A recent All-Party Parliamentary Group on the subject of positive vetting of staff has also pointed out that including service users in recruitment may help to bring about 'a powerful and symbolic change' in the culture of an organisation (Norman Warner, quoted in Crowhurst, 1997).

About the Research Project

The project (funded by the Joseph Rowntree Foundation) set out to address two basic questions: what factors make involvement in staff recruitment likely to happen and how can these factors and good practice be encouraged? It aimed to do this by first evaluating the extent and nature of user involvement in recruiting staff for residential and day services for adults with learning difficulties, then developing guidelines for good practice in this area. Each part of the project had its own objectives.

Part One - a national survey of residential and day care services – aimed:

- to discover to what extent adults with learning difficulties were involved in the process of selecting staff in the private, voluntary and local authority sectors of residential and day care provision in the UK;

- to examine the extent of their involvement at each level of the recruitment process;

- to identify which factors inhibited or promoted the development of strategies for user involvement.

We sent out 471 questionnaires to managers of day and residential services in the private, voluntary and statutory sectors in England, Wales and Scotland. Postal questionnaires for use in the survey were developed in close collaboration with service users. Four discussion groups helped to identify the issues which people with learning difficulties considered should be included in the survey. In all, 182 questionnaires were returned which could be analysed: a response rate of 41%.

Part Two of the project focused on areas which appeared to be examples of high quality or innovative practice. Using a case study approach we set out:

- to document the experiences of people with learning difficulties who had participated in interviewing staff; the views of successful candidates whose interview panel had included at least one person with learning difficulties and the perceptions of senior members of staff involved in the interview panel;

- to evaluate the outcomes of user involvement as perceived by the main stakeholders. (For example, how far do service users' comments actually influence the selection process?);

- to identify features of good practice and make recommendations for policy and practice concerning user involvement in recruiting staff.

We visited eight services across the UK, covering a wide geographical area. The fieldwork included visits to local authority day services and residential services from the private, voluntary and statutory sectors. The sample design ensured that a range of different sizes of homes and day services were approached. We also included a mixture of urban and rural locations and areas where there were significant minority ethnic populations.

People with Learning Difficulties as Recruiters: The General Picture

Our survey of managers of residential and day services in England, Scotland and Wales discovered that 59% of these services had involved people with learning difficulties in staff recruitment on at least one occasion. In the majority of cases, this involvement had been in the most recent appointment, which had almost all been for care or support staff.

There was very little evidence of involvement where management posts were concerned.

Our definition of involvement in the recruitment process was a broad one, ranging from drawing up the job description, through to participating in interviewing and selecting staff. So, although the overall proportion of 'involving' services was quite high, the figures for different stages of the process tell a different story. People with learning difficulties were most commonly participating in planning the interview, preparing the questions, interviewing and selecting the successful candidates:

> *At the Glen Centre in Scotland, people with learning difficulties have played an important role in choosing staff over the past three years. Those interested in the recruitment process can join an 'interviewing group' which meets regularly to discuss, plan and practise relevant activities. Members of this group take turns to join the formal interview panel, which comprises the centre manager, the social work manager and one person with learning difficulties. Candidates are invited to the formal interview only, and each of the three interviewers has an equal vote.*

There was little evidence, however, of involvement in activities such as drawing up the job description, advertising the post and shortlisting candidates.

Yet people with learning difficulties had many useful thoughts and ideas to contribute at these stages. Indeed findings showed that if people with learning difficulties are clear about the sort of person needed from the outset, the whole recruitment process will make more sense to all concerned, as the following quote demonstrates:

> *(We) talked about the qualities. (We) didn't know who was coming for the interview but (we) thought, well we have got say a deputy's position going, so what things do they need to be able to do for that job.* (Day service user)

In about one-third of services, people with learning difficulties were not involved in the interview process at all; their views were sought solely during the informal stage (for example, showing candidates around the home or day service or other similar activities):

> *Residents of number 15 Ashgrove Road, a privately-run group home in the South of England, have the chance to meet candidates as they arrive and to show them around the house. Candidates are then shown into the lounge, where they can drink coffee and chat with residents. After all candidates have been interviewed formally, the home manager asks the residents for their opinions of each person.*

The recruitment process for the majority of 'involving' services included informal activities and/or an interview with service users, as well as an interview with the senior manager and other staff:

> *The Fieldview Centre provides a day service to 80 people with learning difficulties living in a semi-rural area in the South-West of England. The Centre's members' committee has been very active in pushing for participation by members in the running of the service. Four committee members make up the 'client panel', which interviews prospective members of staff. Candidates are invited to meet and chat with people with learning difficulties over a cup of coffee, before their interview. This is followed first by the interview with clients, and then by a second 'formal' interview with the manager and personnel officer. Although members of the second panel are not allowed, formally, to take the client panel's views into account, they do use this information, informally, to help them reach a decision about who to appoint.*

More unusually, a small number of the case study respondents explained that people with learning difficulties were wholly responsible for conducting interviews in their service. As one might expect, the majority of these examples came from independent user-run advocacy groups:

Northshire People First have appointed two new workers over the last 12 months. As an independent advocacy group, members are responsible not only for the day-to-day running of the organisation, but also for the recruitment and employment of the paid support workers. A group of five members volunteered to take part in recruiting staff. With help from the management committee, they designed an easy-to-understand application form, advertised the post, short-listed candidates, and interviewed and selected the best person for the job. This same group of people are now looking at ways of setting up user-led staff supervision.

Benefits of User Involvement

Encouraging people with learning difficulties to get involved in recruiting new staff brings with it many benefits, not just for the service, but for prospective candidates too. Service users are experts at working alongside and getting help and support from staff; it's something they do every day. This expert knowledge can prove invaluable in terms of assessing candidates in an interview situation:

Qualities were quite important, whether they are able to do a job, that's the most important. (Day service user)

Some young folks maybe have a good brain and that, it's not that, it is how we see their values. (Day service user)

Candidates' attitudes towards working with people with learning difficulties and their ability to interact with service users can often come across much more clearly in a recruitment process where service users are themselves involved. The people with learning difficulties we spoke to found it easy to recognise when a candidate was patronising them, or not taking the client interview seriously. It also seemed that people with learning difficulties were asking more direct and sometimes more insightful questions than service managers or personnel officers. The question 'Why do you want to work with us?' requires a clearer and more direct answer than 'Why do you want this job?'. As one day service manager summed up:

It opened my eyes to a lot of people who perhaps would have been excellent in the formal interview, but whose actual interaction with clients was very poor.

For candidates, the process of user involvement was a good way to find out more about the service in which they would be working. It was also a chance for them to get to know the people whom they would be supporting. The fact that user involvement was supported by the service was also a source of information to candidates. As one successful candidate said:

I had a positive image of the home, because people with learning difficulties were involved. It gave me the idea that the job was worth pursuing.

Of course, the converse argument also holds true: user involvement is a good way of discouraging unsuitable candidates. The most important benefit, therefore, is that involving people with learning difficulties should enable better and more suitable candidates to be appointed: the main goal of any recruitment exercise.

Promoting Good Practice

Although the benefits of user involvement in recruitment seem clear, quite a few 'involving' services had experienced some difficulties in getting the process started. These included:

- lack of guidance or training materials

- lack of commitment from managers

- opposition from trades unions and personnel departments

- lack of flexibility within established recruitment procedures

- doubts by staff and service managers over the ability of people with learning difficulties to be objective, maintain confidentiality and keep to equal opportunities practice

- lack of available training for service users in recruitment and fair selection procedures.

The main problems experienced by people with learning difficulties included forgetting what to ask or 'getting stuck'. Although this was a temporary problem for many people, the availability of a good support worker helped to alleviate their immediate embarrassment, as the examples below demonstrate:

All of a sudden my mind went blank. I couldn't see it, I couldn't remember the words, so they had to help me get over that.
(Day service user)

I got stuck at the last minute. I didn't know what to say. Martha (supporter) kept me going. (Day service user)

Other problems included not keeping to the pre-set questions, feeling nervous, and acting subjectively towards known candidates. Our findings showed, however, that with training, practice, and careful and adequate support, most people with learning difficulties could overcome these difficulties and participate successfully.

All of the barriers mentioned above had been surmounted in various ways by services where effective involvement was taking place. In these services, a mixture of the following factors helped to promote good practice:

- pressure for change from people with learning difficulties and a commitment by them to the idea of user involvement

- commitment from staff and support from service managers for implementing user involvement

- the opportunity to work with trades unions and personnel departments in order to set up the recruitment process and to develop appropriate training

- obtaining up-to-date information about how other organisations were involving service users, either as a result of discussion with other services or by reading about recent developments

- willingness to learn from experience, keeping a record of successes and difficulties and to adapt practice accordingly

- involving people with learning difficulties at every stage of the recruitment process and especially in drawing up the job description: this enabled service users to have a clearer idea about the sort of person they were looking for

- effective support from staff who had a good understanding of the recruitment process

- plenty of opportunities for preparation and practice

- training on all aspects of recruitment, including equal opportunities and confidentiality.

Commitment from people with learning difficulties to the idea of user involvement in recruitment was a vital ingredient for successful participation. In services where people had more chances to learn and to practise recruitment skills, and where their views were valued by staff, interest and commitment was much higher.

The findings of our study strongly indicate that good support and the chance to participate in training are the basic building blocks of effective user involvement. This is not a surprising finding; what surprised us more was the realisation that in many services people with learning difficulties were expected to participate in the recruitment process *without* access to these two vital requirements. Thus, only 25% of survey respondents provided recruitment training for people with learning difficulties. When problems occurred in the recruitment process, these were often perceived as being due to an inherent lack of ability by people with learning difficulties. But our findings contradict this view. Where good support and training was available, people with learning difficulties used and understood the concept of confidentiality. Where good equal opportunities training was available and where people had opportunities to practice scoring and assessing candidates objectively, discrimination and bias rarely occurred. As one successful candidate from a local authority day service said:

> *It was very professionally done. They made me feel at ease, but I didn't pick up any clues about what they thought of me. I actually sat with one of the members at lunchtime and she didn't give anything away at all. I thought this was very, very good - it must have been hard not to say anything.*

The right to choose

There was a strong feeling amongst those we talked to that involving people with learning difficulties in the recruitment process was somehow 'morally' right. Respondents were not uncritical of the process; they did not accept the idea of user involvement unthinkingly. There was little doubt, however, that the recruitment process provided an important opportunity for putting self-advocacy skills into practice and that the right to choose was an important one for all service users.

More specifically, many respondents felt that the 'right to choose' was especially relevant when that choice encompassed someone with whom people would be spending a lot of time, even sharing their home with:

> *It's only fair - they have every right to be involved. It is their home, they have to live there and they have to share their house with a member of staff. So in the end it should be their choice.* (Support worker, private day service)

The opportunity to meet prospective members of staff before they started work was seen as a useful process in itself. In this way, user involvement gave clients and staff a chance to get to know each other earlier rather than later:

> *If you are going to be working with a certain person you have got to get to know them. You have got to get on with them. So you have to imagine them working with you.*
> (Day service user)

Such involvement was also a potentially rewarding experience for people with learning difficulties in terms of their own personal development:

> *I thought it was a great experience. You are learning more about it and you are also learning how to deal if you had to do a real interview for yourself. If you were walking into a place and you said I have to go and get this interview, then I think it is about being really punctual and well dressed.*
> (Day service user)

Perhaps the best answer to 'why involve?' is that involving users does actually help more suitable candidates to be appointed. Of the services who had been involving users for some time, all felt sure that the best person for the job had been chosen on each occasion. As one day centre manager summed up:

I have to say that it has been a very positive experience. Clients have been very insightful. I think it is worth saying that we haven't yet had an appointment that hasn't worked out. People who the clients have chosen have all fitted in extremely well. (Manager, local authority day service)

The Way Forward: People with Learning Difficulties as Employers

It is no coincidence that the most successful examples of participation were coming from independent, user-led organisations. Several self-advocacy groups around the UK are now adept at applying for funding from a variety of sources. This funding can then be used, amongst other things, to employ support workers. In these situations, people with learning difficulties are the employers, since the organisations are run and overseen by a management committee, whose members are people with learning difficulties and their allies. As employers, people with learning difficulties are in a position to take full responsibility for the recruitment of new staff, and to have complete influence over who to appoint.

Over the last few years more disabled people have been setting up Independent Living schemes, which allow them to control their own funds to employ personal assistants (d'Aboville, 1995). To date, very few people with learning difficulties have had access to direct or indirect payments (which enable service users to receive cash directly or indirectly from the local authority to organise and buy the kind of support that suits them best), or to the many Independent Living schemes that are being established in different parts of the UK (Holman and Collins, 1997). It is likely, however, that this will change, as people become increasingly dissatisfied with traditional day and residential services.

As employers, people with learning difficulties will need support and advice to equip themselves with the skills and knowledge needed by those who hire and fire staff. The need for training on the recruitment process is merely the tip of a much larger iceberg. With training and support people with learning difficulties can be enabled to deal with a whole range of personnel issues, over and above the recruitment of new staff.

Acknowledgements

This chapter is based largely on material published previously as follows:

Townsley, R. and Macadam, M. (1996a) *Choosing Staff: Involving People with Learning difficulties in Staff Recruitment.* Bristol: Policy Press.

Townsley, R. and Macadam, M. (1996b) Personnel Services, *Community Care*, 3 - 9 October 1996, pp 30 - 31

We are grateful to Community Care and Policy Press for their permission to reproduce parts of this material here. Thanks also to Jenni Lauruol for permission to reproduce her illustrations, which originally appeared in *Plain Facts No. 7* 'Choosing Staff' (University of Bristol: Norah Fry Research Centre).

References

d'Aboville, E. (1995) *Commissioning independent living. A guide to developing personal assistance schemes and support services.* London: Kings Fund.

Crowhurst, G. (1997) Involve service users in recruitment. *Community Living*, p 3. January 1997.

Holman, A. and Collins, J. (1997) *Funding freedom. A guide to direct payments for people with learning difficulties.* London: Values into Action.

Townsley, R., Howarth, J., LeGrys, P. and Macadam, M. (1997) *Getting involved in choosing staff: a resource pack for supporters, trainers and staff working with people with learning difficulties.* Brighton: Pavilion Publishing.

Other resources

'Choosing Staff' *Plain Facts No. 7,* University of Bristol, Norah Fry Research Centre (Summary of the key points from the research for people with learning difficulties; also available on audio-tape).

Margaret Macadam was, at the time of writing, a Research Fellow at the Norah Fry Research Centre, University of Bristol. She has twelve years' experience in research and social policy analysis; recent work has involved assessing the effects of legislation on health, education and short-term care services for people with learning difficulties. Margaret now lives in Christchurch, New Zealand.

Ruth Townsley worked with Margaret on the original 'Who Chooses?' project. She is now working on a new project 'Learning to Choose' again funded by the Joseph Rowntree Foundation which will implement and evaluate service-wide training on involving people with learning difficulties in staff recruitment.

Contact address
Norah Fry Research Centre
University of Bristol
3 Priory Road
Bristol BS8 1TX
England

15 Choice and Control
Making Direct Payments Work for People with Learning Difficulties

Andrew Holman and Jean Collins

Introduction

The Community Care (Direct Payments) Act 1996 makes it possible for disabled people in the UK, including people with learning difficulties, to have a Direct Payment to pay for their community care services. The Department of Health says: 'A Direct Payment is a payment made by a Local Authority to an individual whom it has assessed as needing Community Care Services'. From April 1997, local authorities, through their social service departments, have been able to make cash payments to individuals directly instead of providing the services they have assessed a person as needing. The individual can then use the money to buy or organise the kind of support that suits them best. Previously, people with learning difficulties have usually only had a choice between the services already on offer in their area, or no services at all. This Act therefore has the potential to bring about dramatic changes to existing community care service arrangements.

This chapter is based on research undertaken for the national campaigning group Values Into Action (VIA), supported by the Joseph Rowntree Foundation and published under the title *Funding Freedom* (Holman & Collins, 1997). The research sought to learn from the experiences of people already using early versions of Direct Payments schemes, and to draw these experiences together in a guide aimed at helping local authorities and support schemes successfully implement Direct Payments for people with learning difficulties.

In Northern Ireland implementation of the legislation is mandatory. Authorities there have been given a year's grace in implementing the Act, and must have Direct Payment schemes in place by April 1998. In the rest of the UK, however, local authorities have discretion to decide for themselves whether or not to implement the Act. The impact of the legislation is therefore likely to vary considerably between different local authority areas. Some local authorities plan to move people currently using third party schemes (where money is paid to an independent scheme before being passed on to the disabled person) to a Direct Payment to the individual as soon as possible. They then plan a staged implementation for other disabled people, including people with learning difficulties. In practice, some people with learning difficulties might have to wait a considerable length of time before they can access Direct Payments via suitable support services or schemes.

Local authorities have the discretion to decide which services will be covered by a Direct Payment as well as which individuals can receive one. However, they cannot discriminate between 'groups' of eligible people. A local authority which chooses to implement Direct Payments, therefore, cannot exclude people on the basis of the label it places upon them. Local authorities must not discriminate unfairly between people who want Direct Payments.

Local authorities are required to seek the views of people who use community care services when preparing their annual Community Care Plans. The Department of Health guidance states that this consultation should include people who wish to receive Direct Payments, and local authorities should therefore listen to the views of people with learning difficulties about Direct Payments. However, a central finding from the research was that most people with learning difficulties knew little or nothing about Direct Payments. Their views were consequently uninformed and pointed to a significant need for initial accessible information on Direct Payments.

Making Cash Payments: Experiences So Far

There are currently well over 60 Independent Living schemes, Personal Assistance schemes and Centres for Independent Living established throughout the UK. Such schemes provide a range of back-up support to disabled people who are managing their own personal assistance arrangements through the use of cash payments.

Some local authorities have chosen to support such Personal Assistance or Independent Living schemes. These are generally, although not exclusively, aimed at providing assistance for people with physical impairments. Some of these schemes do support a few people with learning difficulties, in helping people look at what they want and need, and providing information and advice about setting up and running their own support or assistance.

More specifically related to people with learning difficulties are various individualised Trusts and service brokerage schemes. A Trust provides the legal framework for some people with learning difficulties to use cash payments and employ support workers, while service brokerage schemes (which are far fewer in number) usually offer additional skilled workers to help people decide and get the kind of support that they want.

Service brokerage schemes have developed expertise in supporting people with learning difficulties appropriately in the assessment, design and implementation of assistance packages, as well as providing an often-needed advocacy role. Support from service brokerage schemes also includes more skilled help to enable people to look at what they want and need, support in implementing assistance packages, a legal framework to ensure any questions of employment or other liability are met and a quality framework to ensure the desired support is delivered.

It is also possible for people with learning difficulties to manage the cash payments for themselves. Some people are happy to take the money and arrange their support themselves or, more usually, with the help of people close to them. Such help has included, particularly in the case of people with greater support needs, the use of 'circles of support' made up of friends, allies and other supporters, who may form a Trust in the person's name. This provides a route for ensuring that spending remains in the individual's control.

People's Stories

The following stories give accounts of how some people with learning difficulties have been using indirect payments for their services for a number of years. These examples demonstrate how versions of Direct Payments can be used to enable people, even those with extensive support needs, to have control over the money for their services.

Jonathan

Jonathan lives in a house with one other man with learning difficulties. He employs a staffing agency to provide part-time support, and he chose the particular worker he wanted. He is clear about the qualities he requires in staff: he wants consistency and people with whom he gets on well. This is especially important to Jonathan in relation to the personal tasks the worker needs to undertake. His social services department pays the money directly into his bank account, and he chooses how to spend it. Jonathan does not have any support from an Independent Living Scheme but his social worker helps him with bills if necessary. Jonathan also goes to a day centre, provided and paid for by his social services department, with which he is happy.

Mark

Mark lives by himself in rented accommodation. He has 24-hour support from five different workers. As Mark used to live in a hospital his money comes from a health authority. Until recently, that money came via a voluntary organisation which had been contracted to provide community services for a large number of ex-hospital residents. Since April 1997 Mark's money has been transferred to his social services department which continues to make payments to him. Health authorities are not permitted to make payments directly to individuals, but under the Direct Payments legislation money transferred to a local authority for social care purposes can be paid out as a Direct Payment.

Mark has a personal Trust fund. The money for his services is paid into an account set up for that purpose. The account is in Mark's own name, even though he cannot sign his name or make a mark. Some people might think that the extent of Mark's learning difficulties and physical impairments prevent him from being able properly to consent to a Direct Payment. However, his experience with the Trust shows that it is possible for people who have considerable support needs, and who do not use speech to communicate, to have independent control over the money for their services. Mark is able to make his wishes known through his actions and behaviour. If he is not happy with what he is doing or who is supporting him it quickly becomes apparent, if there is someone there who knows how to listen to him.

Mark controls his life by employing an independent broker to help him arrange his support. The broker ensures that Mark is truly happy with the arrangements and support provided and changes them if he is not. The broker is also responsible to Mark's trustees. All know Mark well and have a brief to ensure that the money is used in his best interests. They also have an agreement detailing audit and monitoring arrangements.

Clive

Clive lives with his sister in a bungalow rented from the local authority. For many years he lived with his parents but moved out in a quest for greater independence, whilst still retaining his family ties. Clive had no service for many years as the traditional options available did not suit him. Eventually he was able to have money for his support needs paid directly from the local authority to his personal Trust. This arrangement has lasted several years. His money was recently increased to enable him to live in his own home, and is now supplemented by money from the Independent Living Fund, which give cash awards to disabled people to pay for care services in their own homes.

Originally Clive's payment was made into a separate account in his name. Concerned with the legality of such payments, he had a Trust created for him that included his sister, a family friend and his advocate. Payments now go into the Trust account. They are waiting to see the direction their local authority takes in response to the Direct Payments legislation before deciding on future practical arrangements. Clive has never had any advice from Independent Living schemes; he has relied upon his advocate who has specialist knowledge in Direct Payments and people with learning difficulties.

Tom

Tom uses the services of an Independent Living scheme. The scheme helped him with his community care assessment by putting him in touch with a peer advocate from a local People First group. This changed the focus of his assessment dramatically. It was felt that previously this had concentrated more upon the views of his carer. The Independent Living scheme now assists him to employ support, aimed at increasing his independence, in line with his new assessment.

It is often assumed that only those people with fewer support needs are able to take on Direct Payments, yet the examples above show that this is not so. A Scottish service brokerage scheme involved in the research has also shown that virtually anyone can be supported to control their own support through Direct Payments. This particular project accepts referrals for any disabled person, including people with learning difficulties and those with a physical impairment. The majority of people using the scheme have previously been excluded from traditional services, often because those agencies have not been able to meet the needs of individuals with challenging behaviour.

This service brokerage scheme helps people identify and find ways to meet their perhaps more complex needs, using individualised funding, including personal bank accounts. It does this by supporting self-assessment and enabling people with learning difficulties, together with their allies and supporters, to explore a wider variety of options than may be thought of traditionally. For instance, instead of only suggesting the local day centre a broader range of more suitable activities or support in jobs will be considered. The majority of people might not be thought able to give consent but, like Mark, people's preferences are obtained by a number of means such as 'getting close' to the individual, talking to those who know them well, and trying out a whole range of different approaches.

Who Can Use Direct Payments?

The suitability and appropriateness of a Direct Payment for any individual should be considered as part of their community care assessment. The Direct Payments Act states that 'the Authority may, if the person consents, make ... a payment'. The issue of consent, and in particular capacity to consent, is therefore a crucial aspect of the whole assessment process for people with learning difficulties.

Some local authorities are intending to offer Direct Payments to as many people with learning difficulties as possible. During the course of the research, however, other authorities suggested that they would not put much effort into developing Direct Payments for people with learning difficulties. A fundamental point in the availability of Direct Payments is the perception local authorities have of their role in relation to people with learning difficulties, especially those who need greater support. Where social services departments deny people with learning difficulties the opportunities that Direct Payments afford they are failing to enable and support them to lead an ordinary life as ordinary citizens.

Gaining Control

In their research into user involvement in staff recruitment Townsley and Macadam (1996) found that nearly sixty per cent of the services they contacted already involved people with learning difficulties in some element of staff recruitment (see Chapter 14). Their project came about because local people with learning difficulties said that their need to be involved in choosing staff was 'crucial'. This need becomes even more crucial with a Direct Payment.

The project has produced a resource pack (Townsley et al., 1997) that sets out ways of involving people with learning difficulties in the different stages of staff recruitment. Whilst it focuses primarily on people with learning difficulties using existing services, it has direct relevance for people using Direct Payments. If service users can be involved in the process of thinking about and drawing up job descriptions, advertising, short listing, interviewing and making a final decision about who to appoint then, after all that, the additional process of employment is not such a huge hurdle to overcome. Indeed, functions such as PAYE and National Insurance can be easily devolved to an outside agency if desired, such as an Independent Living scheme.

Several people questioned in our research made accurate assessments of their situation should they use a Direct Payment.

Carl did not underestimate the amount of support he would need to enable him to employ someone. He would need some 'help with advertising, interviewing, recruitment and paying wages'.

Having the right staff is a hugely important matter for people with learning difficulties. Having the right or wrong staff affects every aspect of people's lives and the control, or lack of it, that they have. The quality of support people receive from staff is something on which everyone can comment, whatever means of communication they may use.

Mark's advocate said: 'It was clear that Mark did not manage well with staff who did not know him; just from a medical view they needed certain skills and knowledge to meet his basic dietary needs. Before he had a Direct Payment, these needs were frequently not met'.

Jonathan said that before he had his own money he lived in the group home and that: 'choice depended upon who was on duty'.

Several other people wanted more from staff, particularly greater consistency. Craig complained: 'the residential home used bank rather than regular staff'.

Carl still has to rely on a carer who does everything for him: 'I want to live on my own … I have no choice in the clothes I wear or the food I eat'. Carl wants support to go out with friends and buy his own clothes.

The level of control over staff was felt to be very important. Tom said that he wanted staff who would: '... treat me well; speak to me properly; have an acceptable appearance and be able to solve problems'.

Several people thought they could have avoided many of the problems they had experienced in current services if they had had a Direct Payment. Some, like Jonathan and Mark, had proved it possible.

The Mental Health Foundation has commented that: 'Meaningful activity during the day is one of the most important constituents of anyone's life' (Mental Health Foundation, 1996). Yet, often, under a banner of choice, the appropriate support and information to enable people to make real choices is lacking; people with learning difficulties can actually end up doing very little during the day or in the evening.

Clive found that, by using a Direct Payment, he could ensure that staff supported him in the farming work he wanted to do. They were there day after day, week after week.

Targeting payment to the support that people actually want can prove very effective. In this way, assistance is focused on the individual, and services are not interrupted by staff or service-orientated activities, such as meetings, over which individual users have no control.

Services for People from Black and Ethnic Minority Groups

Some support agencies are now more aware of the needs of people with learning difficulties from black and ethnic minority groups. However, despite the individualised approach advocated in assessment, it cannot be assumed that their needs are being adequately addressed.

A Black People First conference reported: 'It can be difficult for people with learning difficulties who are black. We are treated differently because of our learning difficulty and because of the colour of our skin' (Black People First, 1994). This different treatment has become known as 'simultaneous oppression' or 'double discrimination' (Baxter et al., 1990). It is important to ensure that Direct Payments are offered equally to people from black and minority ethnic groups in ways that are appropriate to them.

This research found very few black people with learning difficulties using current schemes. However, Direct Payments can be extremely useful for people from black and minority ethnic communities, when used imaginatively and flexibly to meet individual needs.

Maria

Maria had lost contact with her family, who came from Italy, when she moved from a long-stay hospital. Individualised funding enabled her to work with a service brokerage scheme to try to find them again. The service broker helped Maria re-establish contact with members of the Italian community in England who remembered her. They were able to obtain her birth certificate, trace family members in Italy, employ an Italian-speaking support worker and ensure support for a holiday to Italy to meet her cousins. Maria has used service brokerage to ensure her support 'recognises the significance of her history, culture and language and one which enables her to develop links and relationships within her community'
(Southwark Consortium, 1997).

The opportunities and empowerment made possible by the use of properly supported Direct Payments should be equally available to everyone. The ability, for example, to employ people of the same faith[1], language or with the desired or necessary cooking skills should certainly provide more

---

1   Legally, disabled people can specify if they want to employ a person from a particular ethnic group. Section 5 of the Race Relations Act allows exceptions when the provision of personal care or when the welfare of the individual may be affected.

opportunities for people to feel acknowledged and supported in their cultural and community identity than they might at present.

Work reported by Simpson and Campbell in Wiltshire suggests that employing staff from black and minority ethnic communities helps. They write: 'In Wiltshire, the personal assistance scheme, WILF (Wiltshire Independent Living Fund), carried out a one year project which employed a personal assistance advisor from an ethnic group to work with people from minority groups. This led to an increase in the number of black people using the support service' (Simpson and Campbell, 1996).

There is still much to be done by services and researchers in addressing these issues. The needs and experiences of disabled people from black and minority ethnic communities interested in or using Direct Payments have not yet been properly explored. It is essential that take-up is appropriately and closely monitored by local authorities and that prospective support schemes clearly address the needs of people with learning difficulties from black and minority ethnic groups.

These issues are also relevant in thinking about other forms of discrimination which might prevent people from taking up Direct Payments or limit their potential use. The research found, for example, an under-representation of women with learning difficulties using the schemes. Yet people might want to use Direct Payments to organise and pay for support that suits their gender, age or sexuality. Assumptions should not be made about what is of value to or 'normal' for any individual.

Conclusions

Unfortunately, Direct Payments are unlikely to be available soon in all local authorities. In one example from the research, a local authority was not intending to offer Direct Payments for at least another year, despite political pressure from its Social Services Committee to implement Direct Payments as soon as possible. It wanted to wait and see first how other authorities fared.

One major shortcoming identified in the research was the provision of effective information. Few disabled people, and even fewer people with learning difficulties, know about Direct Payments. In areas where Independent Living schemes are established there is the chance that those who do use Direct Payments might spread the word about their potential benefits. However, most people with learning difficulties are not involved in such schemes. Consequently, people with learning difficulties have tended to ask their social services department for the provision of better services, rather than for a Direct Payment. It would be easy to interpret this lack of demand as a lack of interest or need, rather than the result of a lack of information.

Traditional methods of disseminating information are of little use to many people with learning difficulties. They need to see how Direct Payments are working in practice. People need to understand how the difficulties have been overcome by others, rather than merely be presented with the potential problems. Direct Payments will stretch current thinking and practice on making information fully accessible. Accessible information should come in a whole variety of ways and certainly means more than buying a symbol translation programme for the assistance scheme computer!

There is an ever-increasing body of evidence showing how the current third party schemes (as close to Direct Payments as the law would previously allow) work. However, most evidence relates to people with physical impairments employing their own personal assistants. Whilst it is very clear that many people with learning difficulties need the same or very similar support, many also need additional assistance, with a different emphasis in the process, to arrange and successfully use a Direct Payment.

Many Independent Living schemes are open to all disabled people whatever the nature of their impairment. Unless people with learning difficulties are supported to use their services, however, they are unlikely to do so. It is striking that, in a recent poll of such schemes, VIA found very few being used by people with learning difficulties and very little involvement by people with greater support needs. This finding was confirmed in the research, with some local schemes saying that they had not really encouraged people with learning difficulties to use their services.

One possible reason for this could be that some local authorities and Independent Living schemes tend to assume that people with learning difficulties will not be able to make use of cash payment either directly or through a third party. The possible use of a third party (where the cash for an individual is paid to an intermediary, like a Trust, on their behalf) may also not be considered. In addition, lobbying by disabled people's groups about Direct Payments over the last ten years, whilst not deliberately excluding people with learning difficulties, has concentrated on meeting the needs of people with physical impairments. Consequently, despite apparently being open to all disabled people, some Independent Living schemes may unwittingly exclude people with learning difficulties, due to the inappropriate nature of their information, support, experience or attitudes. VIA believes that, instead of excluding people with learning difficulties, Direct Payments schemes should address the issue of how to make their services accessible to all.

The place of 'consent' in the Direct Payments Act represents, for the first time in community care legislation, the possibility that a section of the disabled population could effectively be barred from its benefits. The Department of Health guidance accompanying the legislation states that the person must be 'willing and able (with assistance) to manage a Direct Payment' (DoH, 1997). The notion of assistance seems to be lost in the practice guidance, however, which suggests a set of questions that social services departments could ask their clients in order to establish their suitability for a Direct Payment. The proposed questions are actually so difficult that many people would automatically find themselves excluded, with no mention having been made of any assistance being potentially available.

The point at issue here is not whether a person can answer complicated questions but whether the skilled support is available, as necessary, to explore with each individual their responses to particular options. The personal stories recounted in this chapter indicate that all people with learning difficulties can potentially use Direct Payments, and it is therefore important that the issue of ability to consent does not become a stumbling block to their inclusion. Schemes set up to implement Direct Payments need to ensure that everyone wishing to use Direct Payments is enabled to have control in the process. It is not necessary for someone to be able to communicate verbally their approval of support workers before employing them. Such approval can be obtained in a number of alternative ways where people with learning difficulties can express their satisfaction with particular individuals. There are myriad ways and means of finding out what an individual with greater support needs wants, and what they do not want.

With Direct Payments, quality assurance (and control) is placed directly with the individual. They can take their money elsewhere if they are unhappy with the service or they can use their direct buying power to demand a better quality of service. Some people purchase support or services from an independent provider, while others create their own 'service' tailored to their specific needs. This latter option has proved to be particularly useful for those with greater support needs. The experience of people using current schemes is that there has been an increase in the quality of their support and, as a consequence, their lives.

Despite the possible difficulties with the implementation of Direct Payments, the research found examples of good practice and a great many schemes thinking about how to make services accessible to people with learning difficulties. As this chapter emphasises, one answer to enabling people with learning difficulties to use Direct Payments is to provide skilled assistance and to use people who know an individual well. Through such means schemes can and are enabling people with learning difficulties to take an active, indeed controlling, part in the assessment process. People are managing to overcome issues of capacity to consent by skilled communication techniques and a growth in understanding about what people want and what they are saying, not necessarily verbally but by a range of other means. Control is shifting from the professional system to the individual, provided she or he has access to the skilled or expert help they need.

By providing the policies, practice, information and additional support required to make Direct Payments really accessible to people with learning difficulties, local authorities will be implementing the Act in the spirit in which it was passed. As a result, all people with learning difficulties in their area who wish to explore the advantages of Direct Payments will have the opportunity to do so.

The Community Care (Direct Payments) Act 1996 offers the opportunity of truly personalised services and support to enable people with learning difficulties to live the lives they want, in the way they want. There are challenges facing those with responsibility to implement Direct Payments; the road ahead is by no means smooth. Nevertheless, the Act opens the door to one of the most exciting and flexible tools to affect services for people with learning difficulties for many years. We must all ensure that this door is not closed in the face of any person with a learning difficulty who wants to move through it.

Acknowledgements

Thanks to Jenni Lauruol for permission to reproduce her illustrations which originally appeared in *Plain Facts 10*, 'Direct payments for people with learning difficulties', (University of Bristol, Norah Fry Research Centre, June 1997).

References

Baxter, C., Poonia, K., Ward, L. and Nadirshaw, Z. (1990) *Double Discrimination. Issues and services for people with learning difficulties from black and ethnic minority communities.* London: King's Fund/Commission for Racial Equality.

Black People First (1994) *Conference Report.* London: People First.

DoH (1997) *Community Care (Direct Payments) Act 1996. Policy and Practice Guidance.* London: The Stationery Office.

Holman, A. and Collins, J. (1997) *Funding freedom: direct payments for people with learning difficulties.* London: Values Into Action.

Mental Health Foundation (1996) *Building Expectations: Opportunities and services for people with a learning disability.* London: Mental Health Foundation.

Townsley, R., Howarth, J., Le Grys, P. and Macadam, M. (1997) *Getting Involved in Choosing Staff – a resource pack for supporters, trainers and staff working with people with learning difficulties.* Brighton: Pavilion Publishing.

Townsley, R. and Macadam, M. (1996) *Choosing Staff: Involving people with learning difficulties in staff recruitment.* Bristol: Norah Fry Research Centre.

Simpson, F. and Campbell, J (1996) *Facilitating and Supporting Independent Living.* London: Disablement Income Group.

Southwark Consortium, (1997) *Making Changes.* London: Choice Press.

Andrew Holman is an independent advocate and service adviser with basic and post qualifying social work qualifications and over twenty years practical experience supporting people with learning difficulties and mental health problems in a variety of settings. He has been involved in a range of consultancy, research, investigations, service evaluations and court work and is also a project consultant to Values Into Action working on areas of empowerment, parents with learning difficulties and on direct payments. He still retains a practitioner role as an independent advocate and service broker to people using direct payments. He is an associate editor for the journal *Community Living* and has a regular column in MENCAP's magazine *Viewpoint.*

Jean Collins worked with people with learning difficulties for ten years before training as a social anthropologist. She was awarded a D. Phil in 1990 and joined Values Into Action (the national campaign with people who have learning difficulties) the following year as Assistant Director.

Between 1991 and 1993 she carried out a programme of research into the process of resettlement from mental handicap hospitals, producing three books: *When the Eagles Fly* (VIA, 1992), *The Resettlement Game* (VIA, 1993) and *Still to be Settled* (VIA, 1994). She has also studied the relationship between housing and support for people with learning difficulties, published as *What's Choice Got to do With it?* (VIA, 1996). She was appointed Director of VIA in 1994.

Contact address
    Values Into Action
    Oxford House
    Derbyshire Street
    London E2 6HG
    England

16 Partners in Policy Making
Far More than the Object of Policy …

Tara Barenok and Colleen Wieck

For those of us who remember it, analysing sentences for grammar class was a laborious task. Most times it went like this: pick out the subject, pick out the verb, see if there is an object. Basically you tried to answer the question: 'Who did what to whom?' Sometimes, analysing public policy can be the same way. People with disabilities and their families all too often are the objects of policies instead of helping to set the rules (either legislated or agency-set) that govern their lives. In 1987, an idea was developed in Minnesota to rearrange the parts of the policy sentence. 'Partners in Policymaking' was designed to provide leadership training to parents of young children with disabilities and adults with disabilities. The program has been replicated in over forty United States and in the United Kingdom. The lessons and values of the program have applications across social policy areas and across oceans.

What is Partners in Policymaking?

Partners in Policymaking is a leadership training program which teaches what works in disability services and supports to the people who have the most experience with what is needed in systems change - individuals with disabilities and parents of young children with disabilities. This hard won expertise combined with the policy tools and strategies that the program presents are the best formula for ensuring a vision for the future. This vision focuses on the independence, integration, inclusion and productivity of people with disabilities in their communities. The program is typically run or funded by a state developmental disabilities council or funded by a private foundation.

The program has 128 hours of instruction provided over eight weekends, with one weekend session each month. This time commitment ensures that Partners 'learn how to learn.' 'What works' (otherwise known as: 'best practices') are a moving target. Continuous improvement of processes means that a person simply cannot any longer learn what works and keep applying the same model indefinitely. The topics of the Partners programs are general enough so that continuous learning is the aim of the session, not acquiring any specific set of knowledge. The time period between each session ensures that Partners get a chance to practise their skills through homework assignments and incremental work towards the completion of a major public policy project.

Why did it come about?

In 1987, Colleen Wieck, Executive Director of the Minnesota Governor's Council on Developmental Disabilities and Ed Skarnulis, Director of the Developmental Disabilities division at the Minnesota Department of Human Services, were struck by the leadership vacuum among young parents and people with disabilities (self-advocates). The average age of members of national associations on developmental disabilities were creeping steadily upwards. Few if any self-advocates were involved in setting direction for these organisations. The need for parents and self-advocates to learn how to make effective systems change was evident. The gains of the disability movement were at stake.

What are the Quality Principles of the Program?

In order to ensure that the program meets its ultimate outcomes (independence, inclusion, integration and productivity for all Partners and their family members), the design of the program built in quality principles that served this end:

Experiential learning

Partners learn by doing. They prepare and deliver testimony to public officials or their representatives. They practise catching public officials in the hallway and getting their stand on an issue across in few minutes. Both parents and self-advocates benefit from the experience of the other group. They use a variety of different learning methods to acquire a very specific set of competencies.

Diversity

Partners groups are diverse in experiences, disability types, geographic location, gender, racial and ethnic backgrounds, income levels and education levels. Partners learn as much from the experiences of others as from the curriculum.

National speakers

Partners obtain training from speakers who provide a national perspective. These speakers are not inhibited by their roles in the state where the program is operating - either they are from outside the state or their job in the state is to make these specific types of changes.

Best practices

Partners learn about what's possible, not about what they already know - the current system of services and supports in their state or area. They break out of the status quo and ask: 'What if...'

Leadership

Partners acquire knowledge not just for knowledge's sake. They take things they learn and take action for social change. They provide leadership for their communities. It's not about getting the most services for themselves and their families: it's about getting what they need and making sure others have the same opportunity.

Length of time

Funders make a commitment to the Partners programs for a full eight weekend sessions of training. Partners receive 128 hours of instruction over the course of a program year.

Sufficient funding

Funders commit themselves to pay for all the program related expenses (meeting space, meals, accommodations, respite and child care, and travel expenses). This money supports the other quality principles. Without addressing these concerns, Partners can't take the first step towards participating.

Evaluation

Partners and speakers evaluate their experiences with the program. A baseline survey is taken of Partners with six month and long term surveys following graduation. These results are tracked and monitored for long term trends. Changes in the program are implemented based on these assessments.

Not an organisation

Partners is a training program - the real work of graduates is in the community, state and national organisations. The program links them with networks and helps them acquire the competencies needed to succeed. No national database of partners exists. A person can't pay 50 dollars to join. After committing to the program and following through with attendance and hard work, a person is a Partner and goes on to change the world.

What are the Values by which the Program Judges Itself?

A quality Partners in Policymaking program is built on the inherent human rights and responsibilities of people with disabilities. Every aspect of the training program must reflect these values - otherwise the program is not living up to its funder's expectations or the quality principles.

People with disabilities are people first: the disability should come second, if at all. Labelling goes against the point of the program - best practices in disability services. If best practices are always changing, giving someone a static label by which their life is defined will be ineffective at best and highly damaging to the person's ability to define him or herself at worst.

People with disabilities need real friendships, networks and bonds, not just relationships with paid staff. All Partners are entitled to establish the connections with each other and policymakers that they need to succeed at making systems change.

People with disabilities must be able to enjoy full mobility and accessibility that allows active participation in community life. This includes physical accessibility but goes beyond it. Learning methods and program materials must be modified so that everyone has a fair shot of attaining the skills they need as systems-change advocates.

Continuity in the lives of people with disabilities is highly important. This continuity takes place through families and neighbourhood connections. Partners programs reflect this need. Again, Partners is not an organisation to which people can belong and not belong, based on membership dues or other signs of allegiance. It is a continuous presence in the lives of people who have gone through the program, providing the support and tools people need to achieve their personal and systems-change goals.

Dignity and respect of people with disabilities is critical. How can a person expect to succeed at changing policy and systems for the better if they cannot respect the other people who are changing it and who will benefit from its change? This also means that Partners are encouraged to respect themselves and their experiences in ways that they may not have before.

People with disabilities must be in positions to negotiate to have their wants and needs met. These positions may be informal, like serving as an on-call adviser for a policymaker who respects and needs the opinions of a person with experience on disability issues. These positions increasingly have become more formal, with Partners graduates taking on policymaking roles as elected and appointed officials at local, state, and national levels.

Choice is critical for people with disabilities in all areas of their lives. These choices are no more, no less, the same rights that people without disabilities have.

People with disabilities must be able to live in the homes of their choice with the supports they need. Institutions and other settings with large numbers of people living together without input into their living arrangements are the thing most antithetical to best practice in disability services.

Productivity through employment and/or contributions as members of their communities is not only the right of people with disabilities; it is their responsibility. People with disabilities work and succeed in competitive employment when this responsibility is recognised by employers.

What does the Program's Curriculum Look Like?

The curriculum is experienced over eight weekends, with 128 hours worth of instruction for each class of Partners. National speakers provide the training. Logistical and program arrangements are made by a coordinator. Each weekend has certain competencies which Partners will attain in the course of the weekend and through completion of homework assignments. The program covers two broad sets of topics:

Life area topics

As the name suggests, these topics give Partners details on the best practices in how services and supports are provided. The presenters are people who are the best at what they do in the country. For example, an inclusive education expert exposes the class to what works with children and young adults in classrooms. The other life area topics are assistive technology and positioning, competitive employment, and independent living and a home of your own.

Policy and systems topics

Partners learn how to interact with federal, state, and county elected and appointed officials. They learn how to write a letter, prepare testimony and other critical skills to access policymakers and their staffs. These tools are effective and proven strategies that will build systemic change possibilities. Community organising is a critical skill that Partners learn. Parliamentary procedure is also covered, with emphasis on both learning how to follow a meeting in which these rules are used and learning how to use the tools for the meetings that Partners will lead themselves.

In both types of topics, Partners learn in interactive ways such as role playing, group activities and small group discussions. They practise giving testimony before actual legislators and their staffs. They discuss issues and concerns directly with state agency employees in a neutral setting. Homework is assigned and Partners report back on their experiences and impressions so that a multiplier occurs - not only do Partners gain their own perspectives on how the system works but also they are exposed to the perspectives of others. Partners get practice at doing what they continue to do after graduation - advocate on behalf of themselves and their families.

How do Programs Ensure that Competencies are Met?

In Partners programs, there is a three pronged approach to ensuring quality improvement. First, long term evaluations are conducted by external evaluators to compare the activity levels of Partners at a baseline before the program, six months after the program and for up to five years after the program. Questionnaires are mailed to Partners. A high return rate has been experienced by programs that have fully implemented this approach. The results are tabulated and analysed for improvements to the program.

Second, the program coordinators evaluate themselves and are evaluated by the funding source. Most programs evaluate quarterly which is more frequent than most grants made by foundations and other funders. This frequency allows programmatic and logistical issues to be corrected quickly and to the greatest effect for participants.

Third, Partners evaluate presenters and the way the training is delivered after each session. The program coordinator takes these suggestions and adjusts the program accordingly before the next session as needed. Comments on presenters are used to determine who will present the topics for the next class.

What Happens to Partners after the Program?

Partners become systems-change advocates. They use the skills and abilities they have developed to influence policies to make the lives of people with disabilities better. A few Partners graduates have served as Kennedy Fellows in the United States Senate. These people provide the Senate committees that address disability issues, with the critical expertise they need from people who know both how the system works and how to make it better. Several Partners graduates have been elected to local and state positions. Many more have been appointed to boards and commissions that directly set the terms of debate for disability policy. Perhaps most profoundly, there are literally thousands of people in the United States and the United Kingdom who share the same expertise and are able to make their own lives and the lives of others better.

Many states provide Partners with funding for continuing education or opportunities to learn new skills as they go through their systems-change activities. These supports are an important refresher for all who take advantage of them. People need these refreshers to continue to be effective.

What Challenges has the Program Faced?

Two main challenges have faced the program since its inception. These challenges are: involving people of diverse cultures in the program and ensuring quality implementation and replication of the program. The Minnesota Council has evolved strategies to deal with each of these issues.

Since 1992, the Council has funded leadership and cultural diversity projects. The first project evolved out of a request from an African American community leader regarding educating parents about their rights given the fact that African Americans are over-represented in special education and the juvenile system but under-served by family support programs. The second project evolved from the Council's recognition of other unserved groups such as Native Americans and others. Each project involves several meetings over six to eight months to provide parents with information on their children's rights. The baseline surveys from both groups found that few of the parents knew that their child had specific rights to education and other services and supports.

The continuing challenge of these projects is to give these parents enough information so that they can participate in the full Partners program. Each project hopes to not only give people the tools they need to participate or even think about participating in Partners but also to give them some concrete tools they can use immediately.

Ensuring the quality principles of the program has become of increased concern in recent years. The Partners model was carefully crafted over a period of several years. The first replications outside the state of Minnesota ensured that the model would work in a variety of settings and on a range of budgets. However, the continuing challenge of advising close to 50 replications worldwide has revealed two experiences. First, programs have tried to modify the quality principles of the program, sometimes out of an honest desire to improve the program and sometimes out of a need to cut budgetary corners. When this happens they often run up against the problems the quality principle was intended to prevent. For example, some programs have tried to have all in-state speakers present on inclusive education. Unfortunately, the speakers may be limited by the roles they play in the state's education system and cannot present the information the parents need to know to demonstrate the competencies regarding inclusive education. The Partners are frustrated: the speaker is telling them about the system they already know too well instead of best practices. The effort to cut corners actually ends up wasting the program's money and the time of everyone involved.

The technical assistance the Minnesota Council provides to program replications has revealed a second experience. Programs have tried to skimp on the evaluation component. Some programs decided not to track long term outcomes by using an external evaluator. Other programs decided to forgo evaluations of each and every speaker of the weekend, opting instead for getting feedback from Partners only on the main speaker or for taking more informal, on the spot, verbal reviews. In either case, these programs have faced considerable threats to their funding or in extreme cases discontinuation of the program. And without demonstration of effectiveness, who could blame the funders?

In response to this need, the Minnesota Council provides technical assistance to the programs on an as-needed basis. This includes phone calls, email and faxes in the weeks preceding sessions and the beginnings of classes. Coordinators are referred to each other for onsite visits of programs or invited to visit the Minnesota program. In addition, coordinators receive a handbook, including useful forms and instructions on quality replication of the program. This handbook is revised every two to three years to keep up with quality improvements and to give coordinators the most up to date information on speakers and topics. Coordinators are also invited to seminars and academies every year to two years where face to face technical assistance is given. Reflecting the quality principles, the Minnesota Council is constantly evolving new and better ways of helping programs by remaining responsive to their needs.

Where has Partners been Replicated?

Partners programs are currently operating or being planned in 42 United States and Territories. Three states and territories are considering operating the program in the future. Just four states and the District of Colombia have never operated the program. Three others previously operated the program but do not do so at the time of writing. There are six sites planning or operating in the United Kingdom. A program has been funded by UNICEF to begin in the Philippines.

Note

If you are interested in finding out more about Partners in Policymaking in your state or territory or to get additional information on the program, please contact either of the authors at the address below.

For information on Partners in Policymaking in the UK contact:

> Circles Network,
> Pamwell House,
> 160 Pennywell Road,
> Upper Easton,
> Bristol BS5 0TX

Tara Barenok is now working for the Minneapolis Budget Office having previously been a Management Analyst at the Minnesota Governor's Council on Developmental Disabilities. She has worked on quality issues, planning, and human rights connections for the Minnesota Council. Tara also worked for Minnesota Advocates on Human Rights and the International Human Rights Internship Program.

Colleen Wieck is the Executive Director of the Minnesota Governor's Council on Developmental Disabilities. She has worked as a direct services provider for five years, as a researcher for three years, and in her current position since 1981. In addition, she is a consultant, evaluator, expert witness and public speaker. Colleen has also been an active member of several national organizations such as The Association for Persons with Severe Handicaps, the Association of Retarded Citizens - United States, and the American Association on Mental Retardation, as well as several national committees.

Contact address
> Governor's Council on Developmental Disabilities
> 300 Centennial Office Building
> 658 Cedar Street
> St. Paul
> Minnesota 55155
> USA

17 Justice for All?
Advocacy, People with Learning Difficulties, Crime and the Law

Susan Hayes

Over-representation of People with Learning Difficulties in the Criminal Justice System

People with learning difficulties come into contact with the criminal justice system in disproportionately high numbers, compared with their representation in the total population (Hayes and Craddock, 1992). Whilst in the past it has been suggested that this over-representation occurs because people with learning difficulties may have a propensity to commit crimes, the 'innate criminality' explanation has now been abandoned.

Although a very small minority may have an abnormality which may lead to criminal behaviour (such as organic brain damage which causes a person to be very violent) the vast majority of people with learning difficulties, like non-disabled people, have no in-built criminal tendency. Both groups tend to come into contact with the criminal justice system for similar reasons, including poverty, poor social skills, poor anger management, limited ability to foresee the consequences of their actions, inappropriate or difficult relationships with others, lack of life opportunities, disrupted family backgrounds, and a history of having been the victims of violence themselves.

Again, like non-disabled people, only a small proportion of the population of people with learning difficulties comes into contact with the criminal justice system. In the Cambridge health district in Britain, of people with learning disabilities who were known to services in that area, only 2% had come into contact with the law, and none were actually prosecuted for the offences allegedly committed (Lyall, Collins and Holland, 1995).

As people with learning disabilities are not over-represented in the criminal justice system because they are innately more 'criminal', other explanations of their over-representation must be explored (Hayes and Craddock, 1992; Hodgins, 1992). Some people with learning disabilities have a tendency to perform actions which bring them to the attention of police - they may display inappropriate sexual behavior in public, or they may verbally or physically assault others, or they may merely stand and watch children playing in a school yard.

Once apprehended, people with learning disabilities may be not recognised by police as being vulnerable during police interviews, and consequently police may not arrange for a third party, expert in the field of learning disabilities, to be present. While police forces throughout the western world are becoming more adept at recognising people with psychiatric illnesses, the suspect with a learning disability is not often being identified (Hayes and Craddock, 1992; Gudjonsson, Clare, Rutter and Pearse, 1993). Research in Britain indicates that 9-15% of suspects being interviewed by police may have a learning disability; (Gudjonsson, Clare, Rutter and Pearse, 1993; Lyall, Holland, Collins and Styles, 1995), yet the numbers of 'appropriate adults' present during police interviews is dismally low (Palmer and Hart, 1996; Bean and Nemitz, 1995).

Some advocates argue that the identification of an accused person as being learning disabled merely adds a label to that person and has little effect upon the outcome of their court case. The opposing view is that the *lack* of identification may have serious implications for the individual's rights in terms of the conduct of the case. There are significant legal issues pertinent to learning disability to be considered, including competency to stand trial, understanding of the right to silence, voluntariness of confessional statements, defences based on learning disability or mental abnormality, and mitigation in sentencing.

The person's rights in these areas may be further compromised by lack of legal representation. Legal representation has been found to be strongly related to concessionary withdrawals (that is, withdrawing the charge with or without conditions to be fulfilled by the accused), the type and seriousness of the plea, the verdict itself, and particularly the verdict in contested cases (Douglas, 1987). Whilst an Australian study (Hayes, 1993) found no difference between the proportion of disabled and non-disabled defendants who were legally represented (one-third of each group), if an accused person with a learning disability is not legally represented, there is an even greater chance that their disability will not be recognised during the criminal proceedings, and that appropriate legal protections will not be implemented. This chapter will now look at each aspect of the criminal justice process and offer suggestions for advocacy.

The Police Interview

Lack of understanding of the police caution is one factor contributing to the difficulties experienced by people with learning disabilities during police interviews (Gudjonsson, Clare and Cross, 1992). Clare and Gudjonsson (1995) conclude that: 'people with learning disabilities would not be able to use the information in the 'Notice [to Detained persons]' to safeguard themselves in police detention' (p. 113) and therefore may be more likely to confess. Even the new simplified 37 word caution in Britain may do little to assist people with learning disabilities because although the wording is less difficult, the concept of the right to silence itself remains complex.

A series of studies (Gudjonsson, 1990,1992,1993; Clare and Gudjonsson, 1993) indicate that during police questioning, people with learning disabilities may be more vulnerable than non-disabled interviewees because they are more likely to acquiesce (that is, answer questions in the affirmative irrespective of their content), and to be misled by leading questions. Furthermore, Clare and Gudjonsson (1995) suggest, it is possible 'having been misled by the initial questions, people with intellectual disabilities may simply repeat their first answers in responses to subsequent challenges...[and this] apparent consistency may give an incorrect impression that it is safe to rely on what they have said' (p. 115). Thus, the person with a learning disability may begin to remember the 'correct story' more clearly than the actual events.

People with learning difficulties appear to be more likely to make a false confession, because they may be less able to look ahead to perceive the outcome of the police interview (Clare and Gudjonsson, 1995). The people with learning disabilities participating in their study were likely to believe that such a confession could be credibly retracted, and would not be considered as evidence of guilt even if produced in court. Furthermore, they were more likely to believe that after confessing, the suspect could return home, at least until the trial. They thought the suspect's guilt or innocence would be apparent to others, and if he were innocent, he would be protected from the impact of his confession (the study used a male suspect in a short film). Thus, the researchers conclude, the person with a learning disability who is *innocent* of an offence may be most at risk during police interviews because they believe their innocence will be obvious, and they will not have to 'fight for their rights'.

The Offences

Criminal offences committed by people with a learning disability tend mainly to be offences against the person, ranging through nuisance offences, assault, serious assault, sexual assault, to murder or manslaughter. They tend to be under-represented on break and enter offences, drug offences, and driving offences, as well as offences requiring planning, such as fraud (Hayes and Craddock, 1992; Hayes, 1993).

Appearing Before Courts

Nearly one quarter (23.6%) of persons appearing before six local courts in New South Wales, Australia had a standard IQ score of less than 70 and therefore could be diagnosed as having an intellectual disability; a further 14.1% obtained a standard score between 70-79, in the borderline range of 'intellectual ability'. Aboriginal and Torres Strait Islander participants were more likely to have lower standard scores. At two rural courts with a large Aboriginal representation, 36.0% of those appearing before the court obtained a standard IQ score less than 70 and thus could be described as intellectually disabled, while 20.9% were between 70 and 79, in the borderline category of intelligence (Hayes, 1996; Hayes, 1997). The lower scores obtained by Aboriginal and Torres Strait Islanders coming before courts may have in part been related to cultural bias in the tests (although every attempt was made to select tests with minimal cultural bias). A second reason for the lower scores probably lay in the very poor physical health of many Aboriginal and Torres Strait Islanders. In comparison with non-Aboriginal Australians, they score less well on every health parameter; it is likely that their cognitive functioning may be linked to their general poorer health.

A second major finding in this study was that 35.6% of the sample fell below the cut off point on the Mini-Mental State Examination (MSE) which indicates a need for further mental state assessment. This group may include people who have psychiatric problems, who are severely affected by stress, intoxicated by drugs or alcohol, who have difficulty with English language proficiency, and some with an intellectual disability.

Whilst no other recent court cohort study has been located, and the generalisability of these results is therefore unknown, the sample did not differ from the total population of persons appearing before local courts in New South Wales in any manner which would be likely to have exaggerated the proportion of people with an intellectual disability. The results indicate that progression from the police questioning phase to the court appearance phase may be harsher for people with an intellectual disability, that is, of those suspects who are questioned by police, more people with an intellectual disability appear before a court. This in turn has implications for police questioning of suspects with an intellectual disability, and underlines the importance for this group having legal representation and an independent third party present during the police interview.

Prison

Whilst there seems to be an over-representation of people with learning difficulties in prisons in the United States, Australia, Denmark, Canada and some other western nations, forming up to 15% of the prison population (Brown and Courtless, 1971; Denkowski and Denkowski, 1985; Noble and

Conley, 1992; Svendsen and Werner, 1977; Kunjukrishnan, 1979; Hayes and McIlwain, 1988) in Britain the proportion of prisoners with learning disabilities does not seem as great. This may be a consequence of more opportunities for alternative placement in the community, or secure units in the mental health system, into which accused persons and offenders with a learning disability may be diverted (Coid, 1988; Gunn, Maden and Swinton, 1991; Murphy, Harnett and Holland, 1995). This may not always be to their advantage. Placement in a secure unit may be indefinite, whereas a sentence handed down by a court is time-limited; the person knows the release date. Proving that the person is no longer a danger to the community may be more difficult; the person may have to make a case for their release, whereas release is automatic at the end of a sentence in the criminal justice system. Diversion from the criminal justice system may, however, be a better option for the person with a learning disability if there is a system of reviews which ensure that the person is not forgotten or by-passed; sentences are finite; appropriate rehabilitation programs are available; and a gradual lessening of security levels and opportunity for re-integration into the community exists.

The over-representation of people with learning disability in prisons may occur because:

- They may re-offend more frequently, and receive short repeat sentences, resulting in being in prison more often.

- Remanding the person in custody rather than allowing bail into the community, and prison sentences, seem to be more frequent for offenders with learning disabilities. This occurs because of the nature of the offence (often offences against a person rather than fraud or other non-violent crime); their presentation in court; lack of understanding of the nature of the disability leading to fear on the part of the judiciary that people with learning disabilities may be violent and dangerous; or the lack of alternative secure residential placements and community-based sentences.

- They may be more likely to be remanded in custody as a result of previous breaches of bail conditions, lack of resources (financial and residential) enabling them to obtain bail, or inadequate supervisory arrangements which do not satisfy the court's requirements for security and protection of the community.

Dilemmas for Advocates

When a client or family member with a learning disability comes into contact with the criminal justice system, some carers may take the view that 'people with this disability ought not to be charged, or interviewed or sentenced', while others may hold the view that they must take the consequences of their actions, like anyone else. Some carers dismiss any option for special treatment or protection for the person with a learning disability, on the grounds of 'normalisation'. But the principle of normalisation should not be used as an excuse for doing nothing to assist the person with a learning disability who is in trouble with the law. In other contexts, where the consequences are less overwhelming, an inappropriate understanding and over-use of the concept of normalisation may not be too dangerous. For example, a decision to reduce the level of supervision in a household may result in some unhygienic housekeeping, or a minor crisis or two in cooking or shopping. Letting someone with a learning disability take the consequences of involvement in the criminal justice system 'just like anyone else in the community' has far more significant repercussions. Denial of the appropriate protections during police interviews may result in a false confession, and incarceration in prison, for a crime of which the person is innocent.

An area in which the concept of normalisation seems to have taken flight into unreality relates to policy decisions by service agencies to summon police and have a resident charged on every occasion when there is a fight or an outburst which results in minor damage to property. This is not an appropriate interpretation of normalisation. It is not 'normal', for example, when two teenagers in a family have a fight and hit out at each other, for the parents to then call the police and have both young people charged with assault. If a person loses their temper at home and hits the wall, making a hole, it is not normal for other family members in the house to call the police and have that person charged with malicious damage. These kinds of incident are usually handled within the family group: appropriate warnings are given about what might happen if the behaviour continues or escalates, and the family takes steps to make sure the behaviour does not occur again. The consequences for the person with a learning disability when police are called may be out of all proportion to the behaviour which was considered offensive.

Long-term consequences for the service facility need also to be considered. For example, a man with a moderate learning disability, living in a group home, assaults another resident on one occasion, after being teased and during a period of instability in the staffing of the group home. The facility's policy directs that police be called and the resident charged with assault. Police interview the man, he admits the offence and his confession is supported by eyewitness accounts from residents and staff. Staff are now in a position of conflict of interest, supporting this resident in the lead up to and during the trial, whilst at the same time supporting the victim, and giving evidence about the behaviour of both during the trial.

If the alleged perpetrator is found guilty, what choices does the judge have in sentencing this man? He may be sentenced to prison, especially if no other community residential facilities will accept him because of his violence. After the term of his sentence, he will return to the community and eventually accommodation will have to be found for him. Or he may be diverted from the prison system into a secure unit or hospital, and may remain there for an indeterminate period in those jurisdictions where there is no regular review of forensic 'patients'.

After the prison or secure unit term, in the absence of any other appropriate placement, or in a remote region, the perpetrator may be returned to the same group home where the offence occurred. Would this process occur if the person was non-disabled? Has this process taught the perpetrator 'a lesson'? The outcome, the prison sentence, for example, may be so remote from the offence as to render it impossible for the offender to conceive of a link between the two. There may not be an outcome discernible to the 'offender' if a fine is imposed and he has no comprehension of money, for instance. The service providers, the residents of the house, the family members, the perpetrator, and the police, may have undergone the entire process with no gain, significant cost, both economic and emotional, and no change in circumstances which might reduce the likelihood of further incidents. The costs and benefits, as well as the morality of instituting such a process, need to be carefully considered.

In other circumstances, the criminal justice process and outcomes may be appropriate, for example, in the case of a person with a mild intellectual disability who understands the nature of the offence, has some volition in relation to the offending behaviour, and who has a history of repeated offences.

Sometimes, carers have no part in making the decision as to whether a charge is brought. The client may have assaulted someone in a public place, the police have been called, and the process instigated before carers are informed of what has happened.

Practical Actions for Advocates

Policies for service delivery

Inflexible policies developed by service providers which prescribe a standard response to every situation where a client is involved in the criminal justice system create more ethical and pragmatic dilemmas than they solve. Outcomes for victims, perpetrators, family members and staff must be considered in each case, in the light of the circumstances of the case, within the framework of a set of ethical guidelines which the service or advocate considers are important for the clients, the community and the service providers. One ethical guideline, for example, may be that where possible decisions should take into account the outcomes for a person with a learning disability, and the outcomes should not be harsher than for a non-disabled offender. The principle of normalisation does not dictate that people with a learning disability must suffer more than their non-disabled peers. On the other hand, the service providers and advocates must resist the temptation to set themselves up as judge and jury, and handle all offending behaviour 'in house', as was done in the days of the total institutions.

Early intervention for problem behaviours

Provision of services to address potential offending behaviour before clients' involvement in the criminal justice system is a vital part of advocacy. Almost all offending acts are the culmination of many years of challenging behaviour which has not been addressed early, effectively and consistently. In a prospective longitudinal study in New Zealand, a set of risk factors at age five years, and delinquency outcomes at age 13 and 15 were examined (White, Moffitt, and Silva, 1989). Boys designated as being at risk of delinquency on the basis of preschool onset of behaviour problems were found to have more than twice the rate of adolescent delinquency than boys not at risk. Delinquent boys were significantly more likely to be assessed as having lower IQs than were non-delinquents. Boys who had been identified as being at high risk because of their early behaviour problems, but were subsequently non-delinquent, had higher IQ mean scores, suggesting a protective effect of IQ. The IQ/behaviour problem link was not as marked for girls as for boys.

Support for the importance of early recognition and management of challenging behaviours in people with learning disability has come from research which found that intelligence measured as early as three years of age can have a significant correlation with later criminal behaviour (Stattin and Klackenberg-Larsson, 1993). These researchers found that delay in language development, particularly maturity of expressive language and comprehension, rather than stuttering or stammering or other difficulties of articulation, were associated with later criminality, even when socioeconomic status was controlled.

These and similar studies underline the importance of addressing behaviour difficulties when they arise, and not relying on the unrealistic hope that the person with a learning disability will 'grow out of' their challenging behaviour patterns.

Knowledge about the criminal justice system

Inevitably carers will have clients who come into contact with the criminal justice system, so every carer must have a working knowledge of the procedures to be followed, and be able to access expert professionals who can give further advice when necessary. It is important to know whether or not it is possible or essential for a third party to be present during police interviews in the particular area of jurisdiction. If advocates are not sure of their rights to assist the person with a learning disability, then it is important to spend some time, a brief telephone call, or a few hours with an expert, in order to acquaint oneself with the legal position, so that the advocate's actions do not jeopardise the client's rights. Information about legal rights must be obtained from an independent lawyer or advocacy service, as information from the interviewing police may not be accurate. Forensic experience by the author has demonstrated that many New South Wales police are not aware that the Police Commissioner's Instructions state that a third party should be present during interviews with a person with a learning disability.

Police interviews

The *Police and Criminal Evidence Act 1984* (UK) includes special safeguards to protect members of vulnerable groups who undergo police interviews. A significant aspect of these protections is the presence of an independent third party, an 'appropriate adult' at the police station during questioning. Programs are being established, in areas including South London, Sheffield, and Southampton, to ensure that volunteer 'appropriate adults' with experience in the field of learning disability are available to attend police interviews with this client group.

Advocates who are present at police interviews must be clear about their role, especially on the issue of whether they are assisting the police or the client. Cases have occurred where a service provider known to the client has been present, but has acted against the best interests of the client. Because the nature of the offence was particularly horrific, the service provider assumed the person with the learning difficulty had been the perpetrator, and in their attempts to help with the case, overlooked the principle of 'innocent until proven guilty'. The role of the third party during a police interview is not merely to be a passive observer to prevent police intimidation, nor simply to aid in communication. The role is to ensure that the person is aware of their rights, and to indicate to police if the client appears not to understand the police caution or the questions, or is becoming distressed and unable to concentrate, or is acquiescing with police, possibly in order to terminate the interview and be allowed to go home (Clare and Gudjonsson, 1995; New South Wales Law Reform Commission, 1993, 1996). If an aggressive or intimidatory style of police interview is occurring, it is salutary for the advocate to state that if this continues, the advocate will withdraw from the interview. Police are then in the position of defending continuation of an interview without an appropriate third party present, or locating another willing third party. It is important to make this statement audible on the tape recording of the interview.

Community-based Sentencing Options

Advocates act in the best interest of the client by providing realistic information to courts about available options for community-based sentencing. Where an appropriate option does not exist, for example, lack of a sex offenders program for a person with a learning disability, advocates must not lead the court to believe that such a program may be able to be implemented. The court needs to know about realistic options in order to make a decision. When a service provider indicates that a suitable program is available, and then the offender breaches the conditions of their sentence because of the lack of those resources and supervision, in many jurisdictions the court has no alternative but to give a custodial sentence. Thus, the offender with a learning disability is placed in the position of serving a custodial sentence because appropriate community services were not available, even though service providers had assured the court that services would be made available. If the court is clear that the services are unattainable, a realistic community based sentencing option may nevertheless be able to be developed.

The Special Offenders Services (SOS) established in Lancaster County, Pennsylvania provides a model for parole and probation supervision of people with a learning disability (White and Wood, 1992). The staff of SOS in Lancaster County believe that many citizens with a learning disability break the law because they have never been taught society's *consequences* for misbehaviour. The overall goal is to enable offenders with a learning disability to complete their probation or parole successfully. The program is a joint systems model where criminal justice and mental health/learning disability systems have combined their resources. Clients are initially seen on a daily basis, crisis situations are dealt with immediately, and clients are assisted with travel training, job searches, budgeting and banking skills, shopping, and other areas of behaviour which might cause them to breach their conditions. The program has achieved the very low recidivism rate of 5% for its clients over a period of ten years, indicating the significance of this consistent, well-focused approach.

Imprisonment

Prison is sometimes regarded as a viable option simply because no suitable community options can be located. In *R v Clarke*, His Honour stated:

> *Her Majesty's Courts are not dustbins into which the social services can sweep difficult members of the public. Still less should Her Majesty's judges use their sentencing powers to dispose of those who are socially inconvenient. If the Courts become disposers of those who are socially inconvenient the road ahead would lead to the destruction of liberty. It should be clearly understood that Her Majesty's judges stand on that road barring the way* (p. 323).

An important area for effective advocacy is the lobbying of governments to provide the 'missing services', the absence of which condemns people with learning disabilities to custodial sentences.

Where a custodial sentence is thought to be appropriate, advocates are advised to contact the prison system to alert administrators to the fact that the client has a learning disability, so that some form of protection can be considered, if necessary. In the New South Wales (Australia) Department of Corrective Services, separate units for prisoners with learning disabilities have been established in some prisons. Prisoners with a learning disability are admitted to the units only if they are at risk in the mainstream of the prison, and not on the basis of their learning disability alone. This tactic is designed to prevent segregation of those prisoners who would cope in the mainstream without problems. The units are staffed with prison officers who elect to work in these environments, and who undergo special training. A programs officer with expertise in learning disability designs a program for each inmate, in conjunction with the inmate and staff who know him or her most closely. A prison officer is appointed as case officer for each inmate, to be a point of constant contact with the inmate and to monitor progress. Chemical restraint is rarely used, and where possible, inmates are weaned off excess medication, with the cooperation of prison medical officers. Prisoners are involved in programs such as anger management, relaxation, conflict resolution, and activities of daily living including cooking, budgeting and practical literacy and numeracy. A disability coordinator within the department allocates inmates to units, on the basis of clear criteria, so that units do not become repositories for non-disabled but disruptive prisoners. For many prisoners, this has been their first experience in a structured and appropriate environment, where their needs and behaviours have been evaluated and addressed consistently. Levels of psychotropic medication have been significantly reduced, and living skills have improved dramatically in many cases (Rannard, 1996). It is ironic that the 'best' environment experienced by these inmates so far during their lives is a prison environment. Economically, the situation borders on tragi-comedy, because the cost of incarceration in a maximum security environment for these prisoners far exceeds the salary for one, or even two community based support workers *for each person.* If early intervention programs had been implemented, governments would have saved money.

Wider social advocacy

People with a learning disability frequently occupy a position which is alienated from the mainstream of society. Many are deprived of the opportunities for education, vocational training, social and adaptive skills training, behavioural management programs, and employment which are available to non-disabled people. These inequities cannot be overlooked, and contribute to their offending behaviour. A long term aim for advocacy must be to improve the general living situation and opportunities for people with learning disabilities.

Preventing victimisation

People with learning disabilities who commit offences have very often been the victims of offences themselves, especially the offences of physical, verbal and sexual assault, neglect, robbery, and fraud. The case of a young man with a learning disability who sexually assaulted a younger boy illustrates this point. The 'perpetrator' had spent his childhood in a series of institutions where he had been repeatedly sexually assaulted by male staff and older residents. He was unaware of the fact that women and men could have sexual intercourse, just as he was unaware of the fact that sex could be consensual and enjoyable. Perpetrator, or victim?

People with learning disabilities who have been given the opportunity of sex education are less likely to be victims of sexual offences, so this protective mechanism needs to be available to every person.

Education for criminal justice personnel

Without detracting from the real concern felt by many police, lawyers, members of the judiciary, and prison staff for the plight of the person with a learning disability, many members of these professions have little or no training or experience in the area. As a consequence, their best efforts may be counter-productive for the person. The advocate must be as alert for instances of inappropriate over-protection, possibly leading to denial of rights, as for instances of stereotyping, ignorance, brutality and harsh treatment.

Conclusion

People with a learning disability in the criminal justice system often find themselves in double jeopardy. Misunderstood, ignored, deprived and alienated in the community, their 'differences' may cause them to be treated unjustly in the criminal justice system. A major problem is the degree of ignorance manifested by many criminal justice personnel, accompanied by lack of identification of the presence of the condition, and lack of awareness of the difficulties faced by the person with a learning disability. Slowly, criminal justice systems are realising that the over-representation of this group in police interviews of suspects, appearances before courts, and in prisons is unacceptable, with some concomitant awareness of their rights.

The criminal justice arena is a fertile field for advocacy. A determined and articulate advocate can significantly alter the life circumstances of a person accused of a crime, or imprisoned for a lengthy period of time. A young man in New South Wales (Australia) was accused of the murder of his younger sister and found not guilty by reason of insanity. Her death allegedly occurred in the course of an argument about which television program they were going to watch. His indeterminate sentence, first in a juvenile justice institution and later in an adult prison, seemed as if it would never come to an end. No suitable placement in the community could be found for him, where he would be under a level of appropriate supervision acceptable to the court. An advocate devoted years to lobbying Ministers and government departments, until eventually he was released to live as the sole resident in a specially created 'group' home in a country town, and provided with 24 hour supervision and appropriate programs designed to assist him to develop social and work skills. He now lives and works successfully in the community, and other residents have moved into the group home. The level of supervision has gradually been reduced. Had it not been for the efforts of one determined advocate, he would still be in a maximum security prison, with no government agency brave enough to give him a chance in the community.

References

Bean, P. and Nemitz, T. (1995) *Out of Depth and Out of Sight*. London: Mencap.

Brown, B.S. and Courtless, T.F. (1971) *The Mentally Retarded Offender*. Washington D.C.: U.S. Government Printing Office, Department of Health Education and Welfare Publication No. (HSM) 72-90-39.

Clare I.C.H. and Gudjonsson, G.H. (1993) Interrogative suggestibility, confabulation, and acquiescence in people with mild learning disabilities (mental handicap): Implications for reliability during police interrogation. *British Journal of Clinical Psychology*, *32*, 295-301.

Clare, I.C.H. and Gudjonsson, G.H. (1995) The vulnerability of suspects with intellectual disabilities during police interviews: a review and experimental study of decision-making. *Mental Handicap Research*, *8(2)*, 110-128.

Coid, J. (1988) Mentally abnormal prisoners on remand - rejected or accepted by the NHS? *British Medical Journal*, *296*, 78-86.

Denkowski, G.C. and Denkowski, K.M. (1985) The mentally retarded offender in the state prison system: identification, prevalence, adjustment, and rehabilitation. *Criminal Justice and Behavior, 12(1),* 53-70.

Douglas, R. (1987) Do lawyers make a difference? *Australian Journal of Social Issues, 22(4),* 377-389.

Gudjonsson, G.H. (1990) The relationship of intellectual skills to suggestibility, compliance and acquiescence. *Personality and Individual Differences, 11,* 227-31.

Gudjonsson, G.H. (1992) *The Psychology of Interrogations, Confessions and Testimony.* Chichester: John Wiley & Sons.

Gudjonsson, G.H. (1993) Confession evidence, psychological vulnerability and expert testimony. *Journal of Community and Applied Social Psychology, 3,* 117-29.

Gudjonsson, G.H., Clare, I.C.H. and Cross, P. (1992) The revised PACE 'Notice to Detained Persons': How easy is it to understand? *Journal of the Forensic Science Society, 32,* 289-99.

Gudjonsson, G.H., Clare, I.C.H., Rutter, S. and Pearse, J. (1993) Persons at risk during interviews in police custody: The identification of vulnerabilities. *Research Study No. 12,* The Royal Commission on Criminal Justice. London: HMSO.

Gunn, J., Maden, A. and Swinton, M. (1991) Treatment needs of prisoners with psychiatric disorders. *British Medical Journal, 303,* 338-41.

Hayes, S.C. (1993) *People with an Intellectual Disability and the Criminal Justice System: Appearances Before Local Courts.* Research Report No. 4. Sydney: New South Wales Law Reform Commission.

Hayes, S.C. (1996) *People with an Intellectual Disability and the Criminal Justice System: Two Rural Courts.* Research Report No.5. Sydney: New South Wales Law Reform Commission.

Hayes, S.C. (1997) Prevalence of intellectual disability in local courts. *Journal of Intellectual and Developmental Disability, 22(2),* 71-86.

Hayes, S.C. and Craddock, G. (1992) *Simply Criminal, 2nd Edition.* Sydney: Federation Press.

Hayes, S. and McIlwain, D. (1988) *The Prevalence of Intellectual Disability in the New South Wales Prison Population: An Empirical Study*. Canberra: Criminology Research Council.

Hodgins, S. (1992) Mental disorder, intellectual deficiency, and crime. Evidence from a birth cohort. *Archives of General Psychiatry, 49(6)*, 476-83.

Kunjukrishnan, R. (1979) 10-year Survey of Pre-Trial Examinations in Saskatchewan. *Canadian Journal of Psychiatry, 24*, 683-689.

Lyall, I., Holland A.J. and Collins, S. (1995) Offending by adults with learning disabilities: identifying need in one health district. *Mental Handicap Research, 8(2)*, 99-109.

Lyall, I., Holland A.J., Collins S. and Styles, P. (1995) Incidence of persons with a learning disability detained in police custody. A needs assessment for service development. *Medicine, Science and the Law, 35*, 61-71.

Murphy, G.H., Harnett, H. and Holland, A.J. (1995) A survey of intellectual disabilities amongst men on remand in prison. *Mental Handicap Research, 8(2)*, 81-98.

New South Wales Law Reform Commission. (1993) *People with an Intellectual Disability and the Criminal Justice System: Consultations*. Research Report No. 3. Sydney: New South Wales Law Reform Commission.

New South Wales Law Reform Commission. (1996) *People with an Intellectual Disability and the Criminal Justice System*, Report 80. Sydney: New South Wales Law Reform Commission.

Noble, J.H. and Conley, R.W. (1992) Toward an epidemiology of relevant attributes. In Conley, R.W., Luckasson, R. and Bouthilet, G.N. (eds.) *The Criminal Justice System and Mental Retardation. Defendants and Victims*, pp17-53. Baltimore: Paul Brookes.

Palmer, C. and Hart, M. (1996) *A PACE in the Right Direction?* Sheffield: Institute for the Study of the Legal Profession, Faculty of Law, University of Sheffield.

R v Clarke (1975) 61 Cr App R 320 at 323, per Lawton LJ.

Rannard, C. (1996) *Personal communication*. Disability Coordinator, NSW Department of Corrective Services. Sydney: New South Wales, Australia.

Stattin, H. and Klackenberg-Larsson, I. (1993)   Early Language and Intelligence Development and Their Relationship to Future Criminal Behaviour. *Journal of Abnormal Psychology 102(3): 369-378.*

Svendsen, B.B. and Werner, J. (1977)   Offenders within ordinary services for the mentally retarded in Denmark.   In Mittler, P. (Ed.) *Research to Practice in Mental Retardation, Volume I, Care and Intervention,* 419-424, Baltimore: University Park Press.

White, J.L., Moffitt, T.E. and Silva, P.A. (1989)   A prospective replication of the protective effects of IQ in subjects at high risk for juvenile delinquency. *Journal of Consulting and Clinical Psychology 57(6),* 719-724

White, H.R. and Wood, D.L. (1992)   A Model for Habilation and Prevention for Offenders with Mental Retardation: The Lancaster County (PA) Office of Special Offenders Services. In Conley, R.W., Luckasson, R. and Bouthilet, G.N. (eds), *The Criminal Justice System and Mental Retardation. Defendants and Victims,* pp 153-166, Baltimore: University Park Press.

Susan Hayes is Associate Professor and Head of the Department of Behavioural Sciences in Medicine at the University of Sydney. She is well known for her work in relation to people with learning difficulties and the law (especially offenders with learning difficulties) and she has written extensively in this area.   She is a registered psychologist with an established forensic psychology practice, working with offenders and victims with learning difficulties.

Contact address
> Department of Behavioural Sciences in Medicine
> University of Sydney
> Blackburn Building (D06)
> New South Wales 2006
> Australia

18 What Really Matters?
Helping People with Learning Difficulties to Shape Services

Ken Simons

Since services constitute only a small part of the life experience of most users, empowerment is far from being the sole preserve of services.
(Grant, 1997)

Introduction

What really matters to people with learning difficulties? If services are concerned with empowering people with learning difficulties, then this is a crucial question. Will it be the chance for an individual to live in his or her own home (including the choice of with whom he or she shares, if anybody), or will it be a place in a registered home that meets the local authority's registration criteria? Will it be the chance to undertake paid work (perhaps with the support to make a successful claim for the Disability Working Allowance) or will it be a place at a day centre run by an organisation with an *Investors in People* award for its personnel policies? Will it be the active involvement of friends and family in a circle of support, or a key worker with a specific level of qualifications?

Clearly, different individuals (and groups) will have different priorities. However, it is a fairly safe bet that in each pair of choices listed above, the first option posed will be closer to the issues that matter to people with learning difficulties than will the second. The key difference between the two is that the first is expressed in terms of people's *lives* (their relationships, their income, their community), the second in terms of the workings of service organisations.

This is not to suggest that organisational issues are unimportant. Services need to be viable as *organisations* if they are going to provide effective sustainable support. However, ultimately all these organisational issues are really the means to an end. Services exist to support people with learning difficulties. Yet all too often organisational concerns have come to dominate. The kinds of services on offer, and the way they are delivered, owe less to the needs and wishes of people with learning difficulties and more to the needs of organisations that provide them.

For practitioners this might seem a rather discouraging message. However, it *is* possible for services to become far more responsive, even within the current context. But for services to change they need to learn two important lessons. These are:

1. If organisations are going to be more responsive to the concerns of people with learning difficulties, then they are going to have to involve them and their supporters in *all* aspects of services.

2. If services are to be relevant to people's *lives*, then they must be much more outward looking.

By definition both these themes raise questions about the *point* of services. They imply a very different vision of what it means to 'support' people with learning difficulties. Rather than seeing services as a kind of compensation for people unable to function in society (Rioux et al., 1997), they become a device for ensuring that people with learning difficulties have a *place* in society. This is through:

*   enabling people to access their rights as *citizens,* along with assisting them to effectively discharge their responsibilities;

*   seeing individuals in their wider social context, where family, friends and community need to be prime considerations for services;

*   providing people with maximum control over their lives;

- organising assistance on the basis of negotiation not imposed professional assumptions;

- working *with* people rather than doing things *for* them;

- being accountable to people with learning difficulties and their supporters.

The rest of this chapter picks up on the two main themes and explores some of the ways that these related ideas have been put into practice. It draws on a number of separate pieces of the author's work, including:

- a study of complaints procedures in social services departments (Simons, 1995);

- a review of supported living initiatives (Simons and Ward, 1997);

- an evaluation of a tenant participation initiative in supported housing (Simons, 1997);

- a review of the involvement of people with learning difficulties in commissioning and purchasing services (Simons, forthcoming).

The first three pieces of work were supported by the Joseph Rowntree Foundation, while the last was sponsored by the British Institute for Learning Disability.

'Nothing about me without me': involving people with learning difficulties in all aspects of services

'Nothing about me without me', is a phrase much used by the Nottingham group Advocacy in Action, and neatly sums up the proposition that services should seek to involve people with learning difficulties in all aspects of their operations; there should be no 'no-go' areas deemed to be the sole preserve of professionals. Four areas deserve a particular focus: participation in developing an effective strategy for services; active involvement of people in front-line services; involvement in organisational structures and processes; and participation in the monitoring of services.

Participation in Developing a Strategy for Learning Disability Services

Traditionally, 'user involvement' has been focused around the activities of service providers. However, commissioners and purchasers of services have a key role in developing the broader strategy for specialist services, within which the individual providers operate. Commissioners and purchasers are continually making critical decisions which affect the overall direction of services. However, they can often be very distant from the day-to-day lives of people with learning difficulties. Effective user participation can therefore be an important corrective.

Social services departments are required to consult widely on their care plans for community care services. However, the extent to which people with learning difficulties are genuinely involved in this process varies considerably. For example, relatively few authorities produce details of community care plans in accessible formats, yet if people with learning difficulties are going to have a chance to respond, this is a vital first step.

Further, once they have been published, getting authorities to actually change their plans is notoriously difficult. A chance for people with learning difficulties to influence the *development* of plans is therefore critical.

A direct input into community care planning

Concerned about the lack of involvement of people with learning difficulties in an earlier round of community care planning, Hackney Social Services Department established four 'focus' groups with a remit to look closely at different aspects of local services. Each focus group consisted of five or six people with learning difficulties, three or four carers, and two or three professionals, including colleagues form other agencies. Each group met a number of times, carried out visits to services, and produced their own reports. These individual reports were then used to develop the community care plans. The process was complemented by additional discussions with People First.

The self-advocacy organisation

A key part of any strategy has to be to ensure that independent advocacy is flourishing. This might include different forms of support to individuals, like citizen advocacy (see Butler et al., 1998; Simons, 1993), help for people wanting to complain about services (see Simons, 1995), or service brokerage (see Dowson 1995; Dook et al., 1997). However, equally such a strategy ought to encompass support for some form of collective user-led advocacy organisation. Chapter 4 outlines the history of self-advocacy in the US and internationally. While there have been important developments in the UK, the extent of support for the self-advocacy organisation People First within this country remains very variable. In some areas, encouragement to self-advocacy is still limited to service based groupings like student councils. Yet in others, access to funds has enabled independent People First groups to establish offices and employ supporters, which has in turn enabled them to undertake a wide variety of roles.

An expanded role for People First?

Once People First groups are firmly established, with the necessary resources, there is more scope for exploring new avenues of work. While some groups have focused primarily on peer advocacy and supporting the development of self-advocacy locally, others have moved into areas like user-led training and consultancy (see Chapter 7), or service evaluations. One group is even seeking to establish a scheme to help local people access direct payments. These new roles represent important new ways for user-led groups to influence services. Moreover, because they are often income generating, they help secure the long term future of People First groups beyond the initial flush of grant aided funding.

Many of the activities undertaken by commissioners and purchasers are seen as 'technical', yet even when the overall strategic process is in place, there is still scope for the involvement of people with learning difficulties in operational planning and development, whether this is developing service specifications or - as below - selecting providers.

A formal role in provider selection

When the contract for a local day service came to an end, local purchasers (Avon Health Authority) worked with the previous provider to find ways to include people with learning difficulties in the re-selection process. A representative of the local People First group was co-opted to the tender selection panel, as were four users of the existing service, each with their own supporters. They joined two members of the Health Authority, plus two other stakeholders. The process of selection (which included presentations by all the tendering organisations, along with 'taster' workshops) was designed to be both fair to the potential providers and accessible to the people with learning difficulties involved. So, for example, instant photographs were taken at each stage to help remind members of the panel about the different options.

Participation in Front-line Services

Taking the principle of 'Nothing about me without me' seriously means looking hard at *every* aspect of the service to try and find ways to involve people. The day-to-day functioning of front-line services is certainly no exception. All of the following tasks are areas where people with learning difficulties might reasonably claim the right to have a say, whether it is to have more control over what happens, to gain experience, or because many of the tasks are what 'life' is about. The list would include: paying utility bills; shopping for food, clothes, or household items; food preparation and cleaning; choosing houses; decoration and maintenance; selecting staff; developing staff rotas; planning activities; training for staff and others; developing policies; managing budgets and disseminating information.

It is important that assumptions about 'capacity' are not used to exclude individuals or groups. For example, Jones et al. (1997) have pointed out that people with greater support needs often get *less* assistance to participate in household activities than their more able counterparts (a classic case of staff tending to do 'for', rather than 'with'). However, there is evidence that effective staff training in 'active support' can make a significant difference in this respect. People with learning difficulties are a very diverse group. It follows that ways of involving people will have to be equally diverse (see Simons, 1997).

The following example was selected because of the emphasis on people with learning difficulties as contributors as well as recipients of support.

Mutual support

The services provided by the organisation KeyRing are primarily targeted at people with learning difficulties who are not seen as a priority for community care. Besides needing to ensure that its services are affordable, KeyRing wanted to develop an approach which recognised that people with learning difficulties themselves have something to contribute. The result is a low-key service that emphasises mutual *support amongst tenants in the small 'living support networks' that KeyRing establishes. The agreement that tenants sign when they join KeyRing emphasises the importance of tenants playing an active part in the network. Part of the role of the local 'community living worker' is to encourage and facilitate mutual assistance amongst the tenants. This might range from being a good neighbour - taking in milk, doing shopping when another tenant is ill, or re-lighting the central heating boiler (something at which one of the tenants has become an expert) - to providing 'moral support' on the street, or when visiting the local council offices.*
(Simons, 1998a).

Involvement within Organisations

While many service providers have become more attuned to the idea of participation in front-line services, far fewer have come to terms with the idea of user participation within the wider organisation: choosing front-line staff might be a possibility, but helping to choose the new chief executive is almost unheard of. For those prepared to look for opportunities, the possibilities are boundless. In some organisations the emphasis has been on task-based participation, while in others the concern has been to establish participative structures.

A key structural role

So far there are few examples of services for people with learning difficulties that are completely user-led. However, SWALLOW, a small housing and support service in North Somerset, can justifiably claim to come close. The organisation grew out of an 'interest group' for local people with learning difficulties who identified as a problem the lack of local opportunities to leave the family home. More than half the management committee is made up of people with learning difficulties, and people with learning difficulties have been employed as part of the SWALLOW development team. The interests of SWALLOW members have ensured that the organisation continues to explore different options, and indeed people with learning difficulties from SWALLOW have joined researchers from the North Fry Research Centre at the University of Bristol on a field trip to look at French employment opportunities for people with learning difficulties and contributed to the final report.
(Pannell, et al., forthcoming)

Participation in the Monitoring of Services

Part of the role of commissioners and purchasers is to monitor the quality of their services. The range of tools they have for this are varied and include: inspection and registration; the development of service specifications; the development of service standards against which performance is to be measured; contract compliance mechanisms; complaints procedures; audits and evaluations.

This is a considerable task and the way it is done can have a significant impact (for both good or ill) on the experiences of people who use services. Reserving the monitoring of services solely for professionals is doomed to failure; there are simply not enough resources for effective professional oversight of all services. The only viable option is to see the monitoring of services as something that has to be done in partnership with people who use services and their families and supporters. This is partly a practical issue; ensuring that people who use services know what to expect, and how to challenge services when things go wrong, is an important part of ensuring that vulnerable people are protected. However, it is also a philosophical issue. Who should have a say in what counts as a 'good' or a 'bad' service if not the people on the receiving end?

Working with users to improve monitoring

The new local authority in Cardiff had inherited a monitoring and review process, which, although valuable, was felt to place undue emphasis on organisational issues. Members of People First Cardiff and the Vale were recruited to help make the process more focused around issues of importance to people with learning difficulties. Users from eight different services ere involved in a consultation process carried out by People First in collaboration with a facilitator. Both positive and negative aspects of the service were identified along with ideas about what an 'ideal' service would look like. From this process members of People First developed some questions to be used by the review teams (which do sometimes include people with learning difficulties) when evaluating local services.

Keeping a wider vision: ensuring specialist services are outward looking

The small staffed houses and group homes that have become the norm for most new developments are generally an improvement on the old long-stay institutions (see Emerson and Hatton, 1995 for a comprehensive review of the evidence). However, they have their limitations. Most notably, while they may have resulted in people with learning difficulties physically living in the community, they rarely succeed in enabling them to become part of it. Further, the way they are structured and funded means that:

- people have minimal disposable incomes (see Simons, 1998b);

- the reliance on special needs funding mechanisms results in a very considerable short-fall in the number of places needed (see Mental Health Foundation, 1996);

- they remain 'schemes' into which services try to fit people, rather than systems designed around individuals.

If services are going to start being genuinely concerned with people's lives, they are going to have to think much more about two issues in particular: opening up access to a wider range of opportunities and seeing community as a key design principle.

Opening up access to other options

The alternative to 'schemes' involves focusing on individuals and then trying to design more flexible services around each person. Helen Sanderson (Chapter 12) details the kinds of processes involved in person-centred planning. Most involve some kind of attempt to answer our original questions: what really matters to each individual person with learning difficulties and how we can design services in the light of the answers.

However, developing a person-centred plan is very much a beginning, not an end. If services are going to respond to what is needed they are going to have to adapt considerably. For most people the answer to a person-centred plan is unlikely to be a place in a residential care home. Two sets of issues stand out for services here:

The need to involve a whole range of potential stakeholders

Opening up a wider range of options for people will inevitably involve supporting people to access mainstream services, including housing, education and leisure services. Ensuring that the needs of people with learning difficulties are not seen as the sole preserve of specialist services will take some considerable changes in attitudes, policy and practice. Specialist services will need to influence these other services directly. They will also need to support people with learning difficulties to make their views known to these mainstream services. For example, the commissioners in Oxfordshire held a conference to which they invited both people with learning difficulties and their supporters, and also representatives of all the critical local agencies, including the Housing Department and other local housing providers.

The need to develop a range of new skills and experience

Supporting people in a wider range of settings will not be the same as providing residential care. There will be new demands on providers, which will require different skills and knowledge (see Simons and Ward, 1997). For example, an income maximisation strategy is critical in unregistered settings (in residential care everything tends to be rather standardised). Support staff need to have sufficient knowledge of the benefit system to ensure people have enough income not only to survive but to have a decent life. Because KeyRing was able to enlist the help of former Citizen's Advice Bureaux volunteers, they were able to markedly increase the numbers of their tenants making successful Disability Living Allowance claims (Simons, 1998b).

Seeing 'community' as a key design principle in services

If we are serious about supporting people with learning difficulties to lead fulfilling lives, then helping them to sustain and build their relationships - their links with their partners, their friends, their family, their local community - has to become a major concern of services. Location will need to become an important design issue for them. Instead of expecting people to move to where services are, we need to think much harder about enabling people to live close to the people who matter to them. This will involve opening up more extensive housing options, including home ownership (King, 1996; Simons and Ward, 1997).

Where links are already broken, more proactive support for people to make new relationships is needed. This has been one of the least successful areas for services and some fresh thinking is required. David

Felce and his colleagues (Felce et al., forthcoming) argue that some of the skills and experience of supported employment might be transferred to the context of 'leisure services', with a much clearer analysis of potential roles for people with learning difficulties in community organisations and the use of 'natural' supports in such settings (that is, recruiting and training people already in that organisation to act as supporters).

At the same time, there has been increasing interest in 'circles of support' (Wertheimer, 1995).

Building community: circles of support

A circle is a group of individuals who agree to meet on a regular basis to help a vulnerable individual achieve his or her goals. Typically they are made up of friends, family members, people from the local church and other people from the local community, who have got to know the individual one way or another. Circles can and often do include members of staff from services, but in a personal capacity, not as a 'professional'. Circles of support have strong communitarian roots. They assume that it is up to all of us as citizens to work together to build inclusive communities. Circles represent one way of organising and mobilising people who might otherwise have remained only marginally involved in people's lives.

Circles of support are not an alternative form of service, nor are they a resource to be controlled by professionals; they exist alongside services, interacting with them in a variety of ways (e.g. members of a circle might act as advocates for an individual). Circles of support represent a classic dilemma for services. How to relate to something that may well be important to the person with learning difficulties is something to be encouraged on principle and facilitated. Yet they may also be a source of criticism of, and pressure on, services. Establishing effective relationships is the key to working in partnership with people with learning difficulties and their supporters.

Final Words

The aim behind this chapter was both to disseminate ideas and engender enthusiasm, for a radical rethink about specialist services. However, it will not be easy for services to become markedly more responsive in the face of countervailing pressures. The examples given here are meant to offer fresh ideas: they do not represent a total solution. Some have proved one-off exercises, which have not been absorbed into the mainstream. Similarly, there are plenty of examples where considerable effort and resources have been put into 'user participation' exercises which have changed little. Not everything with the label of 'participation' or 'empowerment' is worthwhile; indeed some initiatives have proved to be a distinctly 'disempowering' experience from the point of view of those involved (Lindow and Morris, 1995). If ideas are to be tried, we need to make sure they are implemented thoughtfully and thoroughly followed through. We need to learn how to embed them into mainstream services.

Whatever else, it is clear that services cannot afford to ignore these ideas. Continuing to provide services without gearing them more closely to the concerns of people with learning difficulties cannot be justified. What is more, in the longer term, it cannot be sustained. In the current financial climate specialist services are daily having to 'do more with less'. The *only* viable way to achieve this will be to work as partners with people with learning difficulties and their supporters.

References

Butler, K., Carr, S. and Sullivan, F. (1998) *Citizen advocacy: a powerful partnership.* London: National Citizen Advocacy.

Dook, J., Honess, J. and Senker, J. (1997) *Service brokerage in Southwark.* London: Choice Publications.

Dowson, S. (1995) *Means to control: a review of service brokerage models in community care.* London: Values Into Action.

Emerson, E. and Hatton, C. (1994) *Moving out: the impact of relocation from hospital to community on the quality of life of people with learning disabilities.* London: HMSO.

Felce, D., Grant, G., Todd, S., Ramcharan, P., Beyer, S., McGrath, M., Perry, J., Shearn, J., Kislby, M. and Lowe, K. (forthcoming) *Towards a full life: research on policy innovation for people with learning disabilities.* Oxford: Butterworth Heinmann.

Grant, G. (1997) Consulting to involve, or consulting to empower. In . Ramcharan, P., Roberts, G., Grant, G. and Borland, J. (eds.) *Empowerment in everyday life.* London: Jessica Kingsley.

Jones, E., Perry, J., Lowe, K., Felce, D., Toogood, S., Dunstan, F., Allen, D. and Pagler, J. (1997) *Opportunity and the promotion of activity among adults with severe learning disabilities in community housing: the impact of training in active support.* Cardiff: Welsh Centre for Learning Disabilities.

King's Fund (1980) *An ordinary life: comprehensive locally based services for mentally handicapped people.* London: King's Fund Centre.

King, N. (1996) *Ownership options: a guide to home ownership for people with learning disabilities.* London: National Federation of Housing Associations.

Lindow, V. and Morris, J. (1995) *Service user involvement.* York: Joseph Rowntree Foundation.

Mental Health Foundation (1996) *Building expectations: opportunities and services for people with a learning disability.* London: Mental Health Foundation.

Pannell, J., Simons, K. and Macadam, M. (forthcoming) *Baguettes and bicycles: the impact of work opportunities on the lives of people with learning difficulties in France and the UK.* Bristol: Norah Fry Research Centre.

Rioux, M., Bach, M., and Crawford, C. (1997) Citizenship and people with disabilities in Canada. Towards the elusive ideal. In Ramcharan, P., Roberts, G., Grant, G. and Borland, J. [eds] *Empowerment in everyday life.* London: Jessica Kingsley.

Simons, K. (1993) *Citizen Advocacy: an inside view.* Bristol: Norah Fry Research Centre.

Simons, K. (1995) *I'm not complaining, but..: complaints procedures in social services departments.* York: Joseph Rowntree Foundation.

Simons, K. (1997) *Whose home is this? Tenant participation in supported housing.* Brighton: Pavilion Publishing.

Simons, K. (1998a) *Living support networks: an evaluation of the services provided by KeyRing.* Brighton: Pavilion Publishing.

Simons, K. (1998b) *New Labour, New Deal? The social policy implications of supported living and employment opportunities for people with learning disabilities.* York: Joseph Rowntree Foundation.

Simons, K. (forthcoming) *A seat at the table: involving people with learning disabilities in purchasing and commissioning services.* Kidderminster: British Institute for Learning Disabilities.

Simons, K. and Ward, L. (1997) *A foot in the door: the early years of supported living in the UK.* Manchester: National Development Team.

Wertheimer, A. (1995) *Circles of support: building inclusive communities.* Bristol: Circles Network UK.

Ken Simons is a Senior Research Fellow at the Norah Fry Research Centre. He has had a long-standing interest in the views and experiences of people with learning difficulties, and the way that these are understood and used to shape services. Ken's recent work includes research on complaints procedures, tenant participation, housing and support services, employment and welfare reform.

Contact address

> Norah Fry Research Centre
> University of Bristol
> 3 Priory Road
> BRISTOL
> BS8 1TX
> England